TEACHING NATIVE PRIDE

TEACHING NATIVE PRIDE

UPWARD BOUND AND THE LEGACY OF ISABEL BOND

TONY TEKARONIAKE EVANS

WSU PRESS

Washington State University Press
Pullman, Washington

WSU PRESS

Washington State University Press
PO Box 645910
Pullman, Washington 99164-5910
Phone: 800-354-7360
Email: wsupress@wsu.edu
Website: wsupress.wsu.edu

First printing 2020

Library of Congress Cataloging-in-Publication Data
Names: Evans, Tony Tekaroniake, author.
Title: Teaching Native pride : Upward Bound and the legacy of Isabel Bond / Tony Tekaroniake Evans.
Other titles: Upward Bound and the legacy of Isabel Bond
Description: Pullman, Washington : Washington State University, 2020. | Includes bibliographical references and index.
Identifiers: LCCN 2020025623 | ISBN 9780874223798 (paperback)
Subjects: LCSH: Bond, Isabel--Career in education. | Upward Bound Program
(U.S.)--History. | Indians of North America--Education--Idaho | University of Idaho--History. | Indian educators--Idaho--Biography.
Classification: LCC E97 .E89 2020 | DDC 370.92 [B]--dc23
LC record available at https://lccn.loc.gov/2020025623

ON THE COVER: Ceremonial shirt of the Plateau people, c. 1820s.
Nez Perce National Historical Park, NEPE 8759.
Image used courtesy of the National Park Service.
Cover design by Angela Moody.
FRONTISPIECE: Sketch by Greg Torline of Chief Joseph Trail Big Hole Battleground, 1988. *Private collection of D. Dyer.*

To teachers everywhere

◈ CONTENTS ◈

Foreword

◈ A TRIBUTE TO ISABEL BOND ◈

THIS BOOK is about an extraordinary person who took time away from her life and her own family to help others. Isabel Bond has a passion for helping people. There are many in this world who help others as part of their job or out of obligation, or they help relatives or close friends who have helped them in the past. Isabel is a person who helps others merely because they need help. She helped me see how important it is to get a good education and do my best to succeed in life. As a result, I have been honored and blessed to serve as an elected official for the Nez Perce Tribal Executive Committee for twelve years.

I first met Isabel in the summer of 1977, when I was referred to the Upward Bound program at the University of Idaho in Moscow. I was a struggling high school student who, at the time, did not really care whether I graduated from high school. I was referred to Upward Bound because my grades were not the best. If I did not get my classes in order, a school official told me, I might not be able to graduate on time.

On meeting Isabel Bond, the director of Upward Bound, I saw how dedicated she was to the program, or maybe I should say, how dedicated she was to the students. She took the time to handpick her teachers and staff and make sure they had a heart for working with young people. She made her daily rounds to confirm that students were where they should be and that the instructors and staff were there for the students.

One day I was acting up—not doing what was expected of me. One of the instructors brought me in front of Isabel for discipline, having told me I was probably going to be expelled from the program and sent home that day. Isabel took me aside and, instead of disciplining or yelling at me as I expected, she talked to me. She said, "Bill, don't you know you are a leader, that you can make a difference; and if you do, others will follow?" I just stood there, ready to argue my point or explain how what had happened wasn't my fault. She didn't even bring up the incident; she just told me I was a leader. She not only allowed me to stay in the program but also placed me in some leadership roles.

There were many times when Isabel would encourage students, picking them up rather than punishing or disciplining them. I watched her help students in the program throughout their high school years and then provide them with assistance getting into college. During our college years, she pushed us to do better and never give up. She set up tutoring help and provided other means to keep us in college.

Isabel never wanted any of her students to be satisfied with an associate's or bachelor's degree. After she congratulated you for getting one degree, she would ask, "Now, have you gotten your paperwork in to start work on your next step?" She was always concerned with how you were doing, what you were doing to better yourself, and always with a gentle hand.

Isabel worked with two and even three generations of students, always employing a "you are better than that" type of inspiration. She put her time, effort, and even her personal resources on the line to make sure those around her had an opportunity to better their lives. I hope you enjoy these memories and accounts from those of us who benefited from her help. After you read this book, you will know that Isabel Bond is a very special person, the kind you only come across once in a lifetime. May this book inspire you and future generations to take that chance and further your education. I am glad I had the opportunity to meet Isabel, and I am grateful that she cared enough to make a difference in my life.

—Bill Picard, Nez Perce Vice-chairman

◈ INTRODUCTION ◈

IN 2014, the US Department of Education celebrated the fiftieth anniversary of Upward Bound, a federally sponsored program dedicated to helping low-income and at-risk students attend college. By then, over two million young people had participated in Upward Bound, from inner cities on the East Coast to rural farming communities in the Midwest. From Alaska to Detroit, and many places in between, Upward Bound students come from many ethnic and social backgrounds.[1] What these ambitious students share is a desire for higher education.

Famous Upward Bound participants include Oprah Winfrey; ABC News correspondent John Quinones; Texas judges Raul Vasquez and Belinda Reyes; and Franklin Chang-Diaz, the first Hispanic astronaut.[2] Due to the federal guidelines drawn up at its inception, Upward Bound has benefited at-risk students and those facing financial hardships. A primary requirement is that they belong to the first generation in their family to pursue a college degree.[3]

At the University of Idaho, these prospective students were also required to live within a two-hundred-mile radius of the campus. Due to the proximity of the Nez Perce and Coeur d'Alene Indian Reservations to Moscow, Idaho, this federal guideline meant that a very high percentage of students fulfilling these criteria would be recruited from indigenous communities. As a result, students from an often underrepresented minority group comprising a very small percentage of the overall population found themselves suddenly in the majority among a group of aspiring teenagers on a major university campus.

According to the 2010 Census, Native Americans make up about 0.9 percent of the US population, or 1.7 percent in combination with other races.[4] While the majority now live dispersed in cities, many indigenous people continue to call reservation lands home. Their histories and cultural practices are often overlooked by mainstream society. Upward Bound at the University of Idaho brought students from native and non-native communities together for a common purpose: to reimagine themselves as university students. The interviews in this book show how the self-actualization and acculturation that resulted from their time on campus, on field trips, and in study halls, changed the lives of many Upward Bound students as well as their teachers.

From 1974 to 1991, Upward Bound at U of I on average recruited fifty-five high school students every summer (not including Bridge program students, who were college freshman). Of those fifty-five students, about 64 percent were Native American and 36 percent were non-native. The highest percentage of non-Indians was 49 percent in 1981.[5] As indicated by student profiles in the program's summer yearbooks, Indian students always outnumbered the others.[6] Due to a combination of regional demographics, the distance requirements for student recruiting, and the personal influence of Isabel Bond, Upward Bound was for many years known at the University of Idaho as "The Indian Program." Although non-Indian herself, Isabel kept a ceremonial war lance in her office, and her library contained many books relating to the history and customs of nearby Indian nations, particularly the Nez Perce, since members of that tribe were the most numerous in that Upward Bound service area and therefore comprised the majority of Indian students in the program.

As a young girl, Isabel was introduced by her mother and uncle to members of the Nez Perce Tribe as well as to their language and traditions. Her work with Upward Bound expanded her associations to several other tribes. Due to her particular dedication to the children and young adults in these communities for more than two generations, her legacy is now linked inextricably with the contemporary history of the Native Americans of northern Idaho.

Upward Bound programs around the country can take on the cultural characteristics of a surrounding community, depending on the sensitivity of its teachers to local conditions. Upward Bound is required to provide instruction in core subjects—such as math, English, and science—but the US Department of Education dictates that each service area can have "substantial discretion" in its content and focus. The regulations state that "how they use that discretion could reflect their [director's] assessments of student needs, their resources and capacities, personal or institutional preferences, or other factors."[7]

While the percentages of Indian students varied from year to year, Upward Bound at the University of Idaho possessed from its inception a Native American sensibility, thanks to founder Ed Madsen, a Nez Perce teacher from Lapwai, Idaho. Isabel worked for Madsen at first and in 1973 took over responsibility for the program at U of I, serving as its director for over thirty years.

In 1988, a remarkable year that will be covered later in detail, the program was comprised of 67 percent Native Americans, one of the highest concentrations of Isabel's tenure as program director.[8] Students that year were taken on an immersive journey through the complex historical landscape of the upper Columbia River basin, where the Nez Perce Tribe repeatedly clashed with US troops in the Chief Joseph War of 1877. Also known as the Nez Perce War, this conflict became a focal point in a process of acculturation between Native Americans and Europeans that continues to shape the history of northern Idaho today.

The title of the Upward Bound student yearbook for 1988 is *Taats Timeepnin Tyum*, which translates to "Happy Summer Memories" in the Nez Perce language. During that summer, Isabel and her teachers used the history, conflicts, literature, culture, and traditions of tribes in the region to build classes, study skills, and other curricula that satisfied federal Upward Bound guidelines while also educating students about the often-overlooked Native American history that surrounded them. With over five hundred other Indian nations across the US, perhaps this book can serve as a template for exploring indigenous communities elsewhere and incorporating their histories into mainstream school curricula.

Indian Country is a big place with many stories. I am an enrolled member of the Mohawk First Nations community of Kahnawake, which is only a short drive from downtown Montreal. The indigenous people described in this book were contacted by Europeans about two hundred years later than the Mohawks' first encounter and live four thousand miles to the west, primarily in rural communities of northern Idaho. Only a few generations ago, Native Americans lived isolated from one another in hundreds of disparate communities across North America. Many of them fought for their cultural survival after their religious practices were outlawed and federal legislation was put into place to ensure that Indian lands would one day go to the highest bidder. Despite many reasons for mistrust of Euro-American intentions, education—especially higher education—has played a significant role in helping indigenous communities survive and even thrive in the face of such challenges.

Today, American Indian communities are networking like never before. This could be seen recently as representatives from hundreds of tribes gathered at the Standing Rock Sioux Reservation in South Dakota to resist construction of an oil pipeline under the Missouri River and through lands held sacred by the Lakota Sioux. The groundswell of support received by these "water protectors," as they are called, from cities across the United States and countries around the world has shown that Native American truths and indigenous perspectives remain a significant and compelling aspect of the public debate. I believe that learning and recovering Native American histories and values and communicating them to the rest of the world is vital for our collective future.

Gaining a college education was for me like climbing a ladder that provided a wider perspective on history and life. I will be forever grateful to my teachers for holding this ladder. As a student of cultural anthropology at the University of Colorado, and during my work as a journalist, I have gained a deep appreciation of the wide array of indigenous traditions and values that are practiced on "Turtle Island," the Iroquois term for North America. The Iroquois have a saying that living in two cultures can be as precarious as standing in two canoes at once. What of the young Indian people today who leave their home communities to explore not just two, but many different cultural perspectives from around the world? Is it possible to retain a specific Native American identity while opening oneself up to the many contingencies of the postcolonial era? This was one of the questions I asked myself when I took up this project.

University life challenges students to confront other ways of seeing the world and helps them incorporate those views into a wider framework. Yet, paradoxically, campus life is also a time to define one's self-identity. One of the many discoveries I made while writing this book was that, while expanding Native American students' personal horizons, the Upward Bound experience also served to help form, expand, and strengthen their Native American identities.

Isabel and her staff supported the spirit and dignity of the young people who gave interviews for this book, many of whom went on to become leaders in their home communities. Non-native students at Upward Bound were often left with a new regard for the first inhabitants of the region. All of the former Upward Bound students I interviewed spoke of the inspiration that came from Isabel Bond and her idealistic, practical, and determined team.

While writing this book, I was inspired by examples of dedication to education that went hand-in-hand with explorations of indigenous cultural traditions. Students created Indian regalia, studied treaties, and read about legendary Native American athlete Jim Thorpe. Field trips included visits to many sites in the region that are significant to the Nez Perce Tribe. In addition to lectures on geology by non-Indian professors, students also attended talks by Native American elders such as Horace Axtell.

This project has also expanded my own sense of what it means to be Native American. Last summer, at the Chief Looking Glass Powwow in Kamiah on the Nez Perce Reservation, my wife and I were able to witness the Gourd Dance, which originated among the Kiowas in the Great Plains. Many of the people attending the dance were former Upward Bound students. Some had children of their own who had by then also attended the program.

One of the dancers described how the Gourd Dance began many years ago with a song told by Red Wolf that was passed down through many generations. He said that performing the dance in Nez Perce country resonates in the present day with the tribe's role in helping the US Fish and Wildlife Service reintroduce wolves to Idaho. Wolf reintroduction and salmon recovery have been hallmarks of the Nez Perce nation's dedication to ecological principles. They represent only two of the many ways in which Native American tradition, education, and political influence have come together in the United States in recent years.

This book is about the origins of one educational program that was ahead of its time in this effort due to the influence of nearby indigenous cultures and history. It includes the stories not only of Isabel Bond and her influential family but of her colleagues and many of their students who, empowered by the Upward Bound experience, were able to meet the challenges that lay ahead. May it provide inspiration to a new generation of students, teachers, and scholars who are coming to understand that indigenous perspectives are essential and that Native American history IS American history.

—Tony Evans, June 2020

PART I

THE INDIAN PROGRAM

Chapter 1

◈ GETTING ON BOARD ◈

ON A summer morning in 1975, a peculiar vehicle arrived at the Pi-Nee-Waus Community Center parking lot in Lapwai, Idaho, the administrative center of the Nez Perce Tribe, as several Nez Perce students looked on in disbelief. An old eight-door limousine recommissioned by Isabel Bond, director of the Upward Bound program, pulled up to transport teenagers from around the region to an educational adventure based at the University of Idaho (U of I) in Moscow.

Students accepted into the program—with parental permission—stood waiting to be picked up alongside enough gear for a six-week stay in the dormitories on the university campus, where they would encounter a new level of academic challenge and personal exploration. Lapwai in those days had a ten o'clock curfew and offered few things for kids to do after school or during the summer. For many of these students, stepping into the odd-looking limo meant the beginning of a month-and-a-half-long experience that would change their lives. Each student carried a sleeping bag, if they had one, and either a bag or suitcase filled with clothing, toothbrush, shampoo, and little else.

Before they could make sense of this strange vehicle, an enthusiastic Upward Bound counselor shouted, "Upward Bound, load up!" Isabel Bond's new prized possession was, in fact, a Checker limo nicknamed the "Gray Goose." It would provide Upward Bound with transportation for years to come. In the parking lot, the kids looked at one another, then threw their bags in the back and climbed in. Some sat very low in the seats so as not to attract attention as the vehicle moved on to the next town to pick up more unsuspecting students.

The drive covered much of central Idaho; the program pulled in as many eligible high school students as possible from the Nez Perce and Coeur d'Alene Reservations and neighboring towns. Kids came in from Kooskia, Kamiah, Orofino, Lapwai, Lewiston, Tensed, Plummer, Worley, Mullan, Wallace, and Sandpoint. They included disadvantaged non-Indian students from towns that had suffered the collapse of the mining industry. Many of the kids had been recruited by Isabel and her teachers months earlier as they networked with school counselors. They sought out kids who were falling through the cracks and deserved a chance to better themselves. The group that summer was a diverse collection of aspiring athletes, artists, nerds, and comedians. They were male and female, short and tall, and from Native American and European American backgrounds. By the end of that summer, they would be a tight group of compadres, calling shotgun to ride up front in the Gray Goose.

A SENSE OF BELONGING

Over a thirty-five-year period, many Upward Bound students became familiar with the Bond household, forty-five miles and a world away from home. The Bond family lived in a comfortable two-story house on a hill east of Main Street in an older, established section of Moscow. Above the front door was a carefully carved wooden sign: "The Bond Shelter." Isabel dedicated herself to these young people and brought them into her elegant home. Her husband, John Bond, a University of Idaho professor, worked to correct their Rez English. During "recalls," when U of I Upward Bound graduates of all ages returned to Moscow, female students sometimes camped out downstairs at the Bond house in a large living room area with two bedrooms. If the downstairs was full, the rest camped outside in the yard.

Upward Bound students passing the talking stick, 1993.
Private collection. Photograph by Darlene Dyer.

Whether on campus or at the Bond Shelter, Upward Bound was a place where students were treated with respect and their basic living needs were met. There was no room for cliques. The program gave them time to focus on studies and transcend differences.

The kids grew familiar with the prestigious university campus and came to feel they belonged there. When her Native American students graduated from the University of Idaho, if they got that far, Isabel educated school administrators on appropriate cultural attire and lobbied for the graduates to be allowed to wear traditional regalia for graduation ceremonies.

Upward Bound students overcame personal and academic challenges, often earning college degrees and breaking the cycles of poverty, isolation, and disenfranchisement that resulted from a legacy of colonial conquest, all while celebrating their Native American heritage. The non-Indian Upward Bound students often came away with a new respect for and understanding of the traditions of Idaho's indigenous peoples.

Upward Bounders have become teachers, community leaders, entrepreneurs, and social workers. A second and now third generation of them have attended the University of Idaho. Some serve in capacities that will welcome yet another generation of students to campus for the promise of higher education.

TEACHING AT UPWARD BOUND

"Without the U of I campus, the program would not have worked," said Gail Jensen, who came to Upward Bound as a student teacher from Troy, Idaho, in 1977. She recently retired from teaching. "Isabel succeeded because she took them to this beautiful environment and showed them people who were respectful of education, where they could explore things they knew nothing about. You never had to say, 'Education is important, education is power.' They could see it all around them."[1] Nationwide, 63 percent of Upward Bound programs offer summer residential programs "designed to simulate a college-going experience."[2] Many other programs offer after-school classes and tutoring at participants' regular school locations.

Gail taught three or four basic English classes each summer, teaming up with fellow teacher Darlene (Matson) Dyer to introduce students to the world of literature. After Darlene assumed a study skills teaching position in 1980, Gail and Darlene worked closely together as Upward Bound English teachers for another thirteen summers. While their students took an interest in drama, literature, and science, many of them focused ultimately on what education could do for their tribe.

"The tribes desperately needed health professionals, teachers, and fish and game biologists," said Gail. The teachers wasted no time in bringing the students up to speed in their studies. They spent at least a couple of hours each day on reading and writing. In later years, Gail taught math and science. She also instructed her students in taking and transcribing notes and showed them how to access library resources to research scientific reports. "Using the library's card catalog was a huge step for them," she said. "The fact is that if kids are not reading well by fourth grade, they are likely to struggle with it for the rest of their lives. We were trying to make up in six weeks' time for a half semester of high school classes."[3]

The Upward Bound experience also provided an ideal environment for experimentation on the part of teachers. They used popular culture as a stepping-off point to engage students' creativity and inspiration. Isabel's teachers were part of a new generation that celebrated multicultural values. They were eager to expand their students' understanding of the region's first inhabitants. Working for Isabel Bond made that mission implicit. "All of us are living on Indian land here," said Gail. "It is respectful to know who came before us and lived here for thousands of years. A lot of white kids had no idea who the land had belonged to. The native kids, even though they may have gone to powwows, sometimes had no idea how their history connected to the land. But this story is a part of who we are and what we are in the West."[4]

While teaching at Upward Bound, Gail soon learned how traditional values could run counter to the expectations of mainstream society and the American Dream:

> Reservation kids will value a relationship more than anything else, more than a house and car, or some great financial success. If someone were in need, they would walk away from a class or a job to help. Nothing takes precedence over a friend or relative calling and asking for help. Native American students would also leave school to attend funerals and other ceremonies, or to play a game together or watch a movie.
>
> During the first couple of years, I had to learn to respect their values about responsibility and not place mine upon them. I valued education above all. They may choose that also, but they are not necessarily going to value the things that I value, like a nice little house with a green yard and white picket fence and money in the bank. Some of the native families we worked with had been living in houses for only one hundred years. Often it was a relationship between an uncle or aunt or some other relative that came first.[5]

In 1978, Darlene Matson (later Dyer) left the Midwest for Moscow, Idaho, to take courses leading to an Idaho teaching credential. She had no idea at the time how immersed she would become in the nearby Native American communities. She began by taking classes from Professor Elinor Michel, a former Upward Bound study skills teacher who had pursued her doctorate at the University of Michigan and was by then teaching full-time at the University of Idaho in the College of Education.

"Elinor encouraged me to work at Upward Bound, so I went to meet Isabel Bond in the spring of 1979," said Darlene, who is now retired from teaching and living in Hailey, Idaho. She was intrigued by Isabel's office library, which contained numerous volumes relating to nearby tribes, especially the Nez Perce. "Isabel was charismatic," said Darlene. "Her teaching staff returned again and again each summer, even though I soon learned that she was working everyone nearly to death."[6]

Like most Upward Bound teachers, Darlene and Gail held regular teaching jobs elsewhere in Idaho but traveled to Moscow each summer to teach during Isabel's six-week Upward Bound programs. Many other teachers, counselors, cooks, former students, and other support staff also made that annual trek. Darlene took the job at Upward Bound and subsequently carried on and further improvised on what Elinor Michel had begun. After her first summer of teaching in the program, however, she was so exhausted that she became uncertain about pursuing a teaching career. A principal from a school in nearby Clarkston, Washington, phoned her to say he would hire her on the spot, but she turned him down. Instead, she spent that school year substituting at Moscow High School.

By fall 1981, Darlene decided to pursue a master's degree. She worked for Professor George Canney, serving as a teaching assistant in his Introduction to Reading class and assisting with his research. Darlene's office space happened to be in the same location as the Upward Bound office, so she continued to interact with Isabel and her students. At Isabel's suggestion, Darlene began to read the books in the Upward Bound library about the once-vast Nez Perce homeland, which at one time included the land under the University of Idaho. She learned about the early Presbyterian missionaries, the treaties of 1855 and 1863, and the war fought against the followers of Chief Joseph in 1877, which took place only a century earlier.

"For me this became a very important history," said Darlene. "I thought it was amazing that we would be out there teaching the descendants of Chief Looking Glass and Chief Joseph. Aside from in movies and on TV, I had never actually seen Indians before. I was from Chicago, where I'd only seen wooden cigar-store Indians, and that was it."[7]

Darlene remained reluctant about teaching and about Upward Bound. During her first week on the job at Upward Bound, she discovered just how challenging her new students could be. One evening before dinner, she packed her papers and headed to Targhee Hall for an evening of "study table," eager to help a group of young men prepare for classes. After parking her car and climbing the steps to the dormitory entrance, she heard voices from above and looked up just in time to see buckets full of water and water balloons headed her way from the roof. A group of students who should have been heading to the study table had instead mobilized an ambush to demoralize the new teacher. Shocked, angry, and soaking wet, Darlene simply turned around, walked back to her car, and drove home.

"I wasn't ready for this at all, and it was completely humiliating because I was not in on the game," Darlene recalled, some thirty-five years later. "I went home to think about what I should do. I knew there was a balance I had to keep as a teacher, between knowing your students and being their friend, and keeping enough authority for them to respect you. But something like this was just too much."[8]

Before Darlene could decide how best to respond, a yellow school bus pulled up in front of her house, driven by a stern-faced Isabel Bond. Out stepped a dozen or so young men who mostly looked at the ground as Isabel instructed them in no uncertain terms to make apologies to Ms. Matson. "They walked into my home single file and said they were sorry and then got back in the bus. Isabel then drove them back to campus," said Darlene. That was the end of it, or so everyone thought. "I learned a lot about interacting with kids from Isabel, about showing by example and holding kids responsible for their actions," said Darlene. "But as supportive as she was of her students, she was equally supportive of her staff. I knew from that day on that Isabel had our backs as well."[9]

UPWARD REINFORCEMENT

One of Darlene's jobs involved following up with students during the succeeding school year, traveling to Lewiston and the reservation towns of Lapwai, Kamiah, Plummer, and Worley. She and Isabel made presentations to Nez Perce communities in Kamiah and at the Pi-Nee-Waus Community Center in Lapwai, encouraging parents to continue pushing their kids to read and study. Darlene noted that Isabel also had her make evening visits to the homes of students in Lewiston and Lapwai during the academic year:

> Isabel was determined to not have her students backslide during the school year. When I traveled without Isabel, by myself, I felt more vulnerable, more self-conscious. I wondered what they were thinking when this tall, blue-eyed, blond woman came to their house—probably, "What is this soyappo [white person] doing at my door?"

Pretty soon Darlene was sitting down in kitchens with parents and their children, reviewing pamphlets on study skills. "The students would take out notebooks, and I could see their double-column Cornell note-taking style," she said. She could see that students were practicing skills learned in the summer program.[10]

She pushed herself to talk to these kids, to ask questions and find out who they were: "Kids at that age, of any cultural group, they don't really know how special they are. I didn't appreciate my Swedish heritage at that age. I felt that they needed to realize they were honorable descendants of Chiefs Joseph and Looking Glass. But I also found out they were just like any other kids—rowdy, distracted, curious, and of all skill levels when it came to schoolwork."[11]

Darlene soon learned that Isabel's family had been part of northern Idaho history for six generations, from the time of the Nez Perce War to the contemporary and ever-shifting social landscape of the American West. To understand Isabel's motivation to improve the lives of her indigenous neighbors, one has to know something about her family and the history of the region.

Chapter 2

◈ A LANDSCAPE OF HISTORY ◈

THE JUNE 1982 issue of *National Geographic* features a photograph of Isabel Bond's mother, Lola Clyde, standing amid the stubble of an early autumn wheat field, wearing an apron. Squinting at the afternoon sun from behind a pair of wire-rimmed glasses, the eighty-one-year-old matron offers a freshly baked apple pie to the camera.[1] Lola was one of many people interviewed and photographed for "A Paradise Called the Palouse," an article that describes the lush farmlands, rolling hills, and eclectic history of the region that straddles the Washington–Idaho border north of the Clearwater and Snake Rivers, where Isabel Bond's family has lived since the late 1800s.

Although the map used in the article to delineate the Palouse country includes sixteen hundred square miles of Nez Perce and Coeur d'Alene tribal land, there are no pictures of or interviews with Native Americans in the story. German immigrant sausage makers, a pair of identical twin carpenters, crop duster pilots, female college rugby players, artists, counterculture back-to-the-land sheep farmers, and ice cream social beauty queens are all featured in the story. A black farmer named Frank King, whose parents staked out a homestead in the area in 1910, is featured in a photo of him standing at night in his barn, carrying a basket of chicken eggs. How can it be that within this fascinating collection of characters, not a single Native American was photographed or interviewed for the story, despite the fact that they have lived there for thousands of years and continue to do so today? Why do Indians often remain invisible to mainstream society?

The article does mention, but only in passing, that the Palouse country, including the land under the University of Idaho campus in Moscow, once belonged to the Nez Perce Indians and served as a favorite summer gathering place for other tribes as well. It points out that native people dug camas bulbs there and bred the leopard-spotted horse known as Appaloosa, as in "a Palouse" horse. Yet, reading this informative article about the Palouse, one could be forgiven for thinking that the Nez Perce are extinct, lost to history but for ancient myths and legends and the black and white photographs in museums that are often accompanied by sad stories about war and broken treaties.

Yet Lola Clyde and her daughter Isabel knew differently. The continuing story of the Nez Perce people was waiting then, as it is today, only a one-hour drive south from the Clyde farm, across the Clearwater River and slightly east of Lewiston, at Spalding and nearby Lapwai, the administrative center of a patchwork of remaining Nez Perce-owned reservation lands stretching south and east for hundreds of square miles.

REDISCOVERING TRIBAL HISTORY AND PRIDE

The human history of the area reaches from at least sixteen thousand years ago to the Nez Perce War of 1877 to the present day. It includes ancient cave sites and landscape features from a mythical time when monsters and creatures such as Coyote, the Trickster, and Ant and Yellowjacket set in motion the unfolding drama of the Nez Perce or Nimiipuu—"the people," as they call themselves. The Nez Perce are more visible than many tribes, thanks to the 1,170-mile-long Nez Perce National Historic Trail, established in 1986. The trail stretches from Wallowa Lake in Oregon to the Bear Paw Battlefield near Chinook, Montana, and follows the historic path of Chief Joseph, who in 1877 led eight hundred Nez Perce men, women, and children as they fled the US military on an embattled trek that was closely documented by newspaper reporters as it took place.[2] The

1877 war has become an indelible piece of American history that depicts the plight of a celebrated Native American tribe during the final years of western expansion under the policy of Manifest Destiny.

Thirty-six years ago, Oregon poet and author Kim Stafford visited the Big Hole National Battlefield in Nez Perce National Historical Park, next to Wisdom, Montana. There, at dawn on August 9, 1877, 163 soldiers of the US Army's Seventh Infantry and 33 civilian volunteers attacked 800 Nez Perce men, women, and children encamped in eighty-nine tipis on a grassy bank of the Big Hole River's north fork.

Stafford wrote about his experience at the park in his essay, "A Few Miles Short of Wisdom"—how he passed through the visitor's center, browsed brochures, and followed the self-guided walking tour of the thirty-six-hour siege that led to the deaths of thirty-three Nez Perce warriors and about sixty elders, women, and children. Twenty-nine US soldiers and citizen volunteers also died during the battle. The walking tour included, as it does today, historic markers to illustrate the positions of army soldiers on the attack and of the Nez Perce snipers who held them down.[3]

History, too, seems to be held down here until the writer notices "far uphill at mirage distance, a ribbon shimmered orange from a twig of pine." Upon further inspection, he finds five strands of ribbon in red and blue flickering "half a fathom long from a single branch of the pine where Five Wounds died."[4]

The Nez Perce knew Five Wounds as Pahkatos Owyeen, war mate of Wahchumyus, or Rainbow. Kim Stafford found many older ribbons marking the site where Five Wounds died, left by unseen hands during nighttime ceremonies. The ribbons were fallen and faded by time. In a moment of personal revelation, the author came to realize that Nez Perce culture persists through ceremony. "A century collapsed into this moment of ground," wrote Stafford. "where generations of private celebration grew outward from one story. This square yard of pine duff bound a guest register that could never be tallied, only renewed, only inhabited by the night faithful memory that walked in the form of the people."

A few years later, Kim Stafford met with and taught Upward Bound students in the Wallowa Valley during an extended learning excursion that honored and celebrated the Native American traditions he had been so intrigued by at the Big Hole Battlefield. Isabel Bond and Darlene Matson organized the trip through Nez Perce homelands in 1988 as part of Upward Bound's twentieth anniversary at the University of Idaho.

Isabel grew up hearing stories about the tribes in the area. The apples in the pie that her mother displayed to a *National Geographic* photographer were grown in an orchard on her grandmother's farm, where trees were taking root during the 1877 Nez Perce War. An old Indian trail along nearby Paradise Ridge led to a camas-gathering place. It reached from the Snake River Canyon forests and lava flows, over the rolling hills of the southern Palouse, and traversed the Clyde farm, crossing from reservation lands into an area that has now been developed by the University of Idaho. Isabel's mother visited with the Indians as they passed through, instilling in her daughter respect for native people's history and concern for their livelihood. Isabel eventually took over an educational program that reflected progressive ideals aimed at helping to renew pride in Native American perspectives and cultural values.

"A lot of people have always thought that Indians were just in the way," said Isabel. "But the truth is that they have historically been denied the opportunity to be their best. When you think of the obstacles they have dealt with, it just makes sense that they are true survivors. I have learned that native kids are a great deal more talented and capable than the general public believes they are."[5]

In the two generations since she first came to work at Upward Bound, Isabel has seen a resurgence of Native American pride and self-determination where a century ago frontier wars threatened cultural survival. Her former students, both native and non-native, are helping to replace a regional history marked by intolerance and conflict with one of mutual support and understanding.

Chapter 3

◈ EARLY YEARS AT UPWARD BOUND ◈

UPWARD BOUND programs across the United States differ from region to region, but in some ways they are all alike. The Economic Opportunity Act of 1964 paved the way for Upward Bound, which began a year later as an experimental program that was part of President Lyndon B. Johnson's War on Poverty legislation. The goal was to help students from low-income families get a college education.[1] The theoretical basis for the program was taken from the work of sociologists Richard Cloward and Lloyd Ohlin's differential opportunity theory, which sought to address the problems of juvenile delinquency and gang behavior.[2]

According to the theory, the conditions underlying delinquency could be resolved by implementing social programs in local communities. They rejected the prevailing assumption that delinquency resulted only from the irresponsibility of young people and argued that it was instead a symptom of poverty and the lack of alternative opportunities caused by living in impoverished circumstances. In 1961, Lloyd Ohlin told the *New York Post*, "The boy who joins a gang isn't in a rut. He has aspirations but no place to go with them."

Today, there are nearly a thousand Upward Bound programs in the United States and its territories. In 2016, over sixty-two thousand high school students around the country received services through Upward

Bound. The program supports low-income, first-generation, and at-risk students eager to attend college.[3] For fiscal year 2017, the federal government made a funding allocation of over $312 million for Upward Bound projects nationwide.[4] The investment appears to be paying off with solid results. According to the US Department of Education, 86 percent of program participants graduating in the spring of 2014 enrolled in college later that year.[5]

Isabel Bond and Darlene Dyer recalled that some Native American parents and grandparents resisted the invitation to send their children to school. They were suspicious of a "white education," and how it might further undermine their traditions and sense of community. This began to change in 1968 with the University of Idaho's first Upward Bound director, Ed Madsen, a Nez Perce man from Lapwai who understood the needs and challenges of indigenous students. Before coming to Upward Bound at the University of Idaho, many students had never set foot on a college campus. That first step away from home was a big one back in 1969 for Otis Halfmoon.

"Ed Madsen was an outstanding individual. I had great respect for him," said Otis, now sixty-seven and one of the earliest participants in Upward Bound. "Pride was one of the main things he instilled in us. We learned that education is the answer. We had a choice: to either become educated and be equal to the white man or become his subject."[6]

A non-Indian Lapwai High School teacher named Carl Johnson convinced Otis to enroll in the program. Among his classmates were Mary Slickpoo, Jo Ann Kauffman, Marci Davis, Joe Daniels, Gordon Higheagle, Nancy Broncheau, and Luke and Sylvia Penney, along with students from several other tribes and a few non-Indian students. The sudden high concentration of Indians at U of I during the first years of Upward Bound was out of the ordinary. "I don't think it had happened before," said Otis. "At that time in Moscow, non-Indian kids would drive by whooping at us, yelling for us to go back to the reservation, but this only caused us to stick together, white students and Indians students. We were all Upward Bound students."

Otis acknowledged that he had entrenched ideas about non-Indians as a teenager, but Upward Bound changed this: "I was raised by a lot of old-timers, and I watched how they were treated by others. I learned to show them respect. But I also knew what it was like to be put down by white people. I was proud to know about my tribal history and language, but by the time I came to Upward Bound I was an angry young man."[7]

Otis soon encountered an Upward Bound teacher named Heather Leithoff, who was also proud of her heritage. "She was a proud Scot," recalled Otis. "She sat me down in her living room and made me listen to bagpipe music for about an hour. This taught me that people from many other nationalities are also proud of who they are. Ms. Leithoff told me again and again that I could succeed in whatever I do. These teachers stressed to us that education would allow us to do what we wanted with our lives. Without her, I would never have earned my bachelor's degree. I would not have had the job I have today with the National Park Service. Heather gave me confidence and taught me to believe in myself."[8]

After his first weeks in Upward Bound, Otis's own biases began to break down. "I guess I hated white people at that time. But then I met some of these white kids from Wallace and Kellogg. They came from some very poor families. We got together for skating parties. I realized that, 'Hey, these guys are okay.' I was able to show them my culture and found that they enjoyed it."[9]

RELIGIOUS DIVIDES

Otis and many of his reservation friends had grown up insulated from mainstream society in many ways, attending summer get-togethers at Talmaks Camp, where the six Nez Perce Presbyterian congregations had been gathering since the early 1900s.

"We would load up cattle trucks with Upward Bound students to bring them to Talmaks and take a swim in the Clearwater River on the way," recalled Otis. "Unfortunately, there had been a schism between the Christian Nez Perce and Indian Religion Nez Perce, an either/or situation."[10]

Isabel Bond had learned of this fateful religious schism among the Nez Perce while she was growing up. She also learned as a child about a more general schism within Christianity as a whole that had been brought to the region before she was born. The confusion had left her ambivalent about Christian religious doctrines.

Isabel's grandfather, Daniel O'Connell Gamble, was born in Donegal, Ireland, in 1857 and came to America at age fifteen. After working as an indentured servant to his older brother, who ran the Laurel Hill Presbyterian boys' school in the Haight Ashbury district of San Francisco, Daniel studied the classics and science and decided upon a career in evangelism, at which point he entered the San Francisco Theological Seminary. He graduated from that institution at the head of his class in 1880 and soon endeavored to minister the Gospel to the Nez Perce people. He was immediately commissioned by the Presbyterian Board of Foreign Missions to be their missionary in the new regions of the Northwest. Later that year, he arrived at the Almota Ferry on the Snake River in eastern Washington. By the time he reached Idaho, he was penniless. According to an account of the First Presbyterian Church in Moscow, the "W. H. Ladd Banking Company" of Portland had even supplied the horse and saddle under him.[11]

Charismatic and devoted to his faith, young Daniel had a prodigious memory and could write poetry as well as recite long passages from the Bible. He was quickly ordained at the presbytery of Moscow and promptly went to work, baptizing the wife and two daughters of Duncan Cameron, a man he had met on the ferry ride across the Snake River. "How better to start the record of a frontier ministry than with this initiating rite in the course of soul-seeking evangelism?" wrote a church historian in a pamphlet celebrating the centennial anniversary of the First Presbyterian Church, which Reverend Gamble founded, as the region was said to have changed from "a raw and raucous frontier" to one of "decorous rectitude."[12]

Reverend Gamble established a homestead in the area below a wooded hilltop near Moscow, called Paradise Ridge. He then answered a call to minister in Canada, where he greatly enlarged a congregation at the First Presbyterian Church of Victoria and served as chaplain to the Royal Hospital and the British Columbia Parliament. While giving a talk at Angela College in Victoria, Reverend Gamble met a seventeen-year-old calculus teacher named Isabella Smith, who would become his wife. The daughter of a construction foreman, Isabella carried a depth of knowledge that few could appreciate at the time. In 1884, Daniel and Isabella married and took up residence to Idaho, where Presbyterian missionaries and Catholics had vied with one another for many years over the winning of Native American souls.

Presbyterian minister Henry M. Spalding first brought the Christian faith to the Nez Perce when he arrived on the banks of the Clearwater River in 1836. Yet, according to some historians, Native Americans in the area had already expressed an interest in Christianity. In 1831, four daring Nez Perce men went east to St. Louis in search of the knowledge and power gained by those who followed the Bible.[13] Recent tribal historians have questioned the true purpose of these emissaries, including one noteworthy Upward Bound participant whose story is told in later chapters.

Arriving in Idaho six years after Henry Spalding died in Lapwai, Reverend Gamble came prepared to continue the mission work that Spalding had begun. No doubt he had read about Spalding's first mission to the Nez Perce and of the elder Chief Joseph's early conversion to Christianity, a faith he later abandoned in frustration over white incursions into Nez Perce territory. Chief Joseph had for years been a loyal follower of the Presbyterian faith—until he saw that betrayal was at hand. After realizing that white government officials had been dealing in bad faith, he famously destroyed a copy of the treaty of 1855 and a Nez Perce translation of the Gospel of Matthew and returned to the indigenous traditions of his people in the hope that doing so would help the Nez Perce prevail against the onslaught of European intrusion.[14] The army fought the Nez Perce War of 1877 against his son, also called Chief Joseph, born Hinmuuttu-yalatlat, which means Thunder Rolling Down the Mountain.

When agents and missionaries sought to build more Christian churches in Nez Perce territory, the younger Chief Joseph protested, saying, "They will teach us to quarrel about God. . . . We do not want to do that. We may quarrel with men sometimes about things on this Earth, but we never quarrel about God. We do not want to learn that."[15]

During this period of resistance by traditional, "non-treaty" Nez Perce, the younger Chief Joseph adopted the beliefs of a Wanapum Dreamer shaman and prophet named Smohalla, who regained converts to traditional Native American spirituality and dress. Smohalla promised salvation for those who rejected European culture and returned to native traditions, saying the white man would disappear from the land.[16] By the time Reverend Gamble arrived in Idaho, the non-treaty Nez Perce had been beaten in the 1877 war and exiled to reservations in Oklahoma and the Colville Reservation in Idaho, far from their traditional homeland in the Wallowa Valley.

Although Isabel Bond's grandfather died several years before she was born, her mother told her that Reverend Gamble had decided not to preach to the Nez Perce because he saw that his ministry was more desperately needed elsewhere. "My grandfather was educated by the King of England to teach other than the Catholic religion," said Isabel. "He had plans to preach to the Nez Perce. But the story I always heard growing up was that he took one look around and decided that the whites in Moscow needed his help, and the help of the Lord, more than the Nez Perce did."[17]

Children find out innocently enough about the biases carried by their parents and grandparents. Isabel discovered one St. Patrick's Day that not all Christians are alike. "My sister asked my mother if there was something green she could wear to school for luck, and to keep from getting pinched," said Isabel. Lola responded, "Your grandfather would roll over in his grave if he heard you say that." She explained to her daughters that her father, the Reverend Daniel O'Connell Gamble, had been decidedly Protestant and therefore Irish orange rather than Catholic green.[18]

This battle for souls between the Church of Rome and the Protestant churches that began hundreds of years earlier in Europe was imported to the American western frontier. The Nez Perce and other tribes were sometimes caught in its skirmishes. To overcome the language divide and make their case for spiritual superiority, early Catholic missionaries in Nez Perce country employed a graphic illustration to win souls: priests displayed a tree diagram with the Catholic Church of Rome at the top of the tree. The other denominations, including Spalding's Presbyterians, were represented as branches on the tree, mere tributaries of the one true church.[19]

By the time Isabel was attending grade school, it had become apparent to Lola Clyde that church activities would not be a priority in her daughter's life. Isabel learned to ride horses and work sooner than she learned to read. "I remember being scared to death at Sunday school because I had not memorized what St. Mark or St. Luke said, or other details from the Bible," Isabel recalled. "Many of the other kids had lived in town and gone to kindergarten ahead of me, and they knew all the answers. At times I would run from the classroom in tears."[20]

Isabel's personal humiliation led to compassion and understanding for the academically challenged students she served during her long career at Upward Bound. Despite her family's deep connection to a local congregation, she does not attend church on Sundays and takes a more secular and practical rather than doctrinal and religious view toward life. "Quoting scripture has little relationship to being a good person," she said.[21]

The issue of religion can still be divisive among Indian nations, yet Upward Bound students like Otis Halfmoon said the differences became less important while in the program: "The thing about Upward Bound is that it brought us all together, whether you were white or Indian or practiced Christianity or the Indian religion."[22]

CULTURAL COHESION

Native American cultural expressions were celebrated from the earliest years of the program. During the summer of 1969, Otis and several friends, along with Ed Madsen, set the stage by challenging the University of Idaho's policy against gambling to allow for traditional stick games among the Indian students. "We loved to play this bone game, a gambling game. It includes various songs and is so ancient, from a very long time ago," said Otis.[23]

Ed organized a delegation of students to approach the university president's office, seeking to declare the Upward Bound dormitories "temporary reservations" for the six-week program. "They gave us approval. We would play girls against boys. They discouraged us from outright gambling, but we did it on the side anyway," he said.[24]

That summer, Ed's Upward Bound program organized a Cultural Days event, which consisted of a mini powwow at the campus arboretum. Groups came from the Nez Perce and Coeur d'Alene Reservations. Otis was part of a drum group composed of Upward Bound students, including Frank Penney, Frank Weaskus, Fred Major, and Joe Daniels. Native American family members came to campus to mix with non-Indian families. Tribal dancers in regalia, including many who were not in the Upward Bound program, danced to the singing and drumming.

Otis came from a prominent Nez Perce family, so how he comported himself on campus was significant. His father, Richard A. Halfmoon, served on the Nez Perce Tribal Executive Committee for thirty-two years, from 1952 until 1984, and as its chairman for sixteen of those years. In his early years, he worked for the Civilian Conservation Corps and as a policeman at the Fort Lapwai Sanitorium; during World War II, he served in the US Army in the South Pacific, Italy, Germany, England, and France.

Otis's mother, Nancy Jackson Halfmoon, graduated from Lapwai High School and was one of the first Native Americans to attend Lewiston Normal School. A full-blooded member of Chief Joseph's Wallowa band of Nez Perce of the Colville Confederated Tribes, Nancy was a founding member of the Chief Joseph and Warriors Memorial Powwow in 1977 and became a member of the Lapwai Prayer Warriors in her later years. While her husband was serving overseas during the war, she worked as a riveter in the Portland, Oregon, shipyards.

Clearly, Otis Halfmoon had a legacy to live up to. Yet, kids being kids, he also took part in his share of shenanigans. "One of the counselors—a Blackfeet guy named Pete Whitford—I used to give him a hard time because the Nez Perce and Blackfeet had tussled long ago over the buffalo hunting areas in Montana. Well, one night my friend Travis Moody and I wanted to stay out late, but we knew that the dormitory doors were locked at ten o'clock. We made a plan to keep the door from locking by sticking a Three Musketeers candy bar in the door jamb."[25]

Otis and Travis slipped out into the night to explore downtown Moscow. "After we got tired and couldn't find anything to do, we came back to the dorm, but the door was locked. It was cold out, so we started pounding on the door, but no one came. I looked in the window, and there was Pete Whitford eating my candy bar, just smiling at us." Pete had decided to teach them a lesson and let them spend a night outside, so the boys walked, shivering, back to town. They eventually found one building that was open. "Catholic churches were open twenty-four/seven, so we opened the door and went inside," said Otis. "We found some carpet back behind the pews to sleep on. It wasn't too comfortable, but it was warm. In the morning, we got up early and made it back to campus for breakfast."[26]

On another occasion, Otis and Travis went to town with two female friends, looking for something to do. "This long-haired hippie-looking guy rode by on a bicycle, asking us if we wanted to buy some marijuana. I said, 'Sure, how much?' He said, 'Twenty dollars.' So, we put our money together to buy this little baggie of stuff and then didn't know how to smoke it. Someone said we should get some rolling papers, so someone went into a store and bought some. We rolled up some joints and lit it up and smoked and smoked, and nothing happened."[27]

The boys returned to campus and stashed what was left of their marijuana safely out of sight in one of the dorm rooms. Their plan was to dispose of it after classes. Otis ran into another Upward Bound student on campus a few days later. She told him the police were up in the boys' dorm. "I walked up there, and it turned out they were waiting for me. Only the police were laughing at us. They said, 'You wasted your money. That was alfalfa you were smoking.'"[28]

The boys were taken to Ed Madsen, who raked them over the coals. "He lectured us big time," said Otis. "He told us how much trouble we could have been in, and all about how marijuana could have hooked us for life. He knew my father was tribal chairman, but he thankfully didn't say anything to him about what had happened."[29]

Isabel followed Ed's lead in incorporating Indian culture into the Upward Bound curriculum. She began in 1969 as an assistant in the program, teaching home economics, drawing on her college studies and practical skills to create a sewing project. "We made vests, which are part of the regalia worn by natives," she said. "I had twenty-five young men and women all making vests in my class. This was very popular because vests are a part of the men's dress for powwows. I selected this project because it was something simple that could be completed in a short period of time, something the students could certainly find success with."[30]

Upward Bound students had a lot to learn, not only about academics and studies, but also about social interaction, self-esteem, and a new set of expectations placed upon them in classes. White and Native American students together learned about their similarities and differences, and how to work and play together.

Just as the program was up and running, tragedy struck. During the fall of 1972, Ed Madsen was hunting in the Frank Church–River of No Return Wilderness when he was accidentally shot in the leg and bled to death before he could get medical help. The assistant director, Bud Langdon, was in charge of the program for a short while but soon departed.

Isabel had gotten to know her students and their relatives while working as support staff, traveling to their home communities to learn about the challenges they faced. In the process, she began to remember some of the Nez Perce words she had learned as a child from her Uncle Gus at her mother's farm. "It just all started coming back when I started working with these kids," said Isabel. The following year, Everett V. Samuelson, dean of the College of Education, looked to Isabel for help with the fledgling program. "Dean Samuelson finally appointed me as director and then supported me at every turn for many years to come. Upward Bound was still new to the university, so I and everyone else still had a lot to learn," Isabel recalled.[31]

FOCUS ON ACADEMICS

The intensive six-week session at the heart of Upward Bound's summer program included instruction in mathematics, laboratory sciences, composition, literature, and foreign languages, as well as the all-purpose study skills classes. The program also included tutoring, counseling, mentoring, cultural enrichment, and work-study programs. Upward Bound students would be the first in their families to go to college. They were also at-risk children or from low-income circumstances.[32] The students could be homeless, in foster care, or aging out of the foster care system and in need of someplace to go. Many of them came from chaotic homes where drug and alcohol use had undermined the family structure.

Chris (Mahoney) Meyer joined the first Upward Bound class at the University of Idaho from 1968 to 1972. Her mother was from the Coeur d'Alene Tribe. Her father was an Irishman from New York City who worked in construction. Although Chris was a cheerleader and active in campus affairs at Plummer High School, she said she always felt disconnected and did not have many close friends. "Upward Bound had a profound impact on my life," Chris commented, "It planted a seed. Back then, there were no counselors meeting with us to discuss college. It was not part of the conversation in my household or in high school. Only Upward Bound could provide us with these possibilities."[33]

During her high school years, her father was drinking heavily. The family dysfunction this created added to other challenges on campus. "It was difficult," she said. "It was a very different time back then. Non-natives received white lunch tickets, but native students received green lunch tickets with 'INDIAN' written on them. My brothers were told they could not date white girls. I think because of the racism that existed on the reservations, we were continuously reminded that we were different. We internalized this idea that we were less than white kids, that we were not as capable. Even today, there are low expectations for native students."[34]

A successful student, Chris was elected homecoming queen her senior year, but this distinction was discredited by some of her classmates, who said the only reason she was chosen was due to the high number of Native Americans on the football team.

The six-week Upward Bound experience afforded her an opportunity to explore new social situations and develop a new perspective on her tribal identity. "That first year was a turning point for me," she said. "I was born and raised on the reservation, so simply being able to walk that campus was a big opportunity. I enjoyed meeting other natives immensely, including a lot of Nez Perce students. Having that shared experience was very important. It helped us to form our native identities." Chris's father, who worked outside of Moscow in construction, would stop by to visit during her six-week program each summer. "I had never had that kind of experience with him before," said Chris.[35]

The Native American staff members hired by Isabel to work in the dorms provided some familiarity for the students. "We had loads of fun in the dorm," said Chris. "I had a non-native roommate and a native roommate. There were some tussles on the floor, but we would just ignore them. It felt safe. Whether you were native or not, what you had in common was poverty. I don't think our high schools taught us how to write. We learned how to diagram sentences but not really how to write."[36]

Upward Bound mentors often helped students discover and develop their talents. During her freshman year at North Idaho College, Chris formed a friendship with Virginia Tinsley Johnson, one of her Upward Bound teachers who had gone on to teach college English. Tinsley became an important mentor to Chris. "Knowing Virginia during my freshman year made a big difference. I felt more secure knowing she had experience with Upward Bound and knew about some of the deficits we

Teaching wolf recovery: Jack Zachary, holding antenna; Sean Shelley, with tracking device; Dan Davis, teacher. *From the 1992 Upward Bound yearbook. Photograph by Darlene Dyer.*

were dealing with. She saved me, really. I was able to get through English, but not because I was skillful at it. Math was also very challenging."[37]

Chris received a two-year degree in education from North Idaho College and attended Gonzaga University in Spokane before completing her bachelor's degree from Eastern Washington University. She was then hired to teach at the Coeur d'Alene Tribal School during her student teaching period: "Even during my four years in college, I felt like I was just surviving. You are so young and working through so much at that time in your life. You have a native identity, and you are also in a non-Indian place. You have those messages playing in your head about being Indian. You don't realize that other non-native students are also struggling. It was a messy time. Not until I was working as a teacher and working toward my master's degree did things settle down for me."[38]

Chris Meyer completed a master's degree in special education and in 1989 was preparing to complete her doctoral dissertation in educational administration. It was the one-hundredth anniversary of the University of Idaho, and Dean Samuelson was on her dissertation committee. Chris was hard at work on a project close to her heart. Her thesis involved interviewing tribal leaders to find out how they maintained their tribal identities while completing college degrees. "I learned that Dean Samuelson was very interested in my success," she said. "I had been told that I did not need a doctorate, but I felt that if I was going to work with people who are working at the university level, I wanted to have the same credentials as my colleagues."[39]

Chris was surprised to learn that she was the first Coeur d'Alene tribal member to receive a PhD. "I honestly did not know until Isabel Bond told me," she said. "My father lived long enough to appreciate what I had accomplished. My mother did not really understand what it meant, what earning a PhD was all about." Chris Meyer now oversees the Coeur d'Alene Tribe's Department of Education. She said many of those Upward Bound students from the first class of 1972 went on to complete college degrees. "We are still a large part of one another's lives," she said.[40]

LIVING IN TWO WORLDS

Chris Meyer and Otis Halfmoon were members of a generation that came of age during a revival of Native American activism on college campuses as well as reservations. Education in legal matters and the sciences would have a profound impact on many tribes in the years to come. During the 1990s, the Coeur d'Alene Tribe fought the State of Idaho and won a US Supreme Court case that acknowledged the tribe's ownership of the south end of Lake Coeur d'Alene. For Chris, this effort represented an expression of age-old cultural values:

> I have never liked all of that Hollywood movie language about Indians worshipping nature, but I just love listening to our men talk about protecting our homeland, about re-introducing the trout to Lake Coeur d'Alene, about protecting the beaver and preserving the waters. It is not just talk. Our tribe lives and breathes this truth. Learning the necessary math, science, and engineering skills early on allows us to be a part of preserving our homeland. I began teaching because I did not want to hinder the younger generation's possibilities. I found only recently that the views that our ancestors are always speaking about were lying dormant in me. Education has helped pull this out. My work as a teacher has allowed this to come forth. It is exciting for me today to know how meaningful is the work of our tribe.[41]

Otis Halfmoon had a similar experience, although his involved working for the US government for twenty-seven years.[42] After Upward Bound, he joined the army and later held numerous positions with the Nez Perce Tribe before earning a certificate as a pharmacy technician and landing a job at St. Joseph Regional Medical Hospital in Lewiston. He kept earning college credits here and there until in 1991 he completed his bachelor's degree at Washington State University (WSU) in Pullman.

As an employee of the federal government, he was stationed from 1991 to 1994 at the Big Hole National Battlefield, Bighorn Canyon National Recreation Area, and Nez Perce National Historical Park; more recently he worked for the National Trails Intermountain Region (now National

Trails) of the National Park Service. He then supported Native American involvement in the National Park Service while working in its Office of Relevancy, Diversity, and Inclusion. "It is important to live in two worlds," said Otis. "We can walk that fine line between academia and being who we are. Native American cultures are all unique, and that is okay whether we are Pawnee, Shawnee, Nez Perce, or from somewhere else."[43]

Chapter 4

◈ MOVING FORWARD ◈

UPWARD BOUND'S survival at the University of Idaho depended on following federal regulations and successfully recruiting students from the surrounding region. Keeping them in the program required both creativity and sensitivity. Isabel and her staff were visited each summer by a US Department of Education employee from Washington, DC, who looked in on classes to confirm that the teachers were complying with federal requirements. Isabel made sure to enforce the program rules to ensure its success.

"I would come to the dorm at breakfast and then at dinner, and then I would be there at the front door for study table after dinner. If they were late, I made them do more time at study table in their respective dorms," she recalled.[1]

After the summer sessions were over, Isabel traveled to high schools within two hundred miles of Moscow to follow up on her students in Lapwai, Plummer, Coeur d'Alene, Kellogg, Wallace, and Kamiah. She met with school counselors and social workers to identify students who were struggling to see if she could do anything to alleviate problems they were having. "Oftentimes we would recruit students while we were there. Or we would come back in the spring," she said.[2]

Isabel dedicated herself to learning about the challenges each student faced at home. She often found these challenges to be generational and significant; but after all, these were the kids that Upward Bound was designed to help. She was determined to find teachers who could contribute to the Upward Bound curriculum in ways that would continue to inspire Native American kids in particular, and in the process she learned that they had not always been taught to value their native traditions in the public schools of their home communities. She set about remedying that situation as best she could at the U of I campus.

UNDERSTANDING THE CHALLENGES

In 1975, Lucinda George was a twenty-three-year-old Nez Perce woman studying for a degree in criminal justice at Lewis-Clark State College (LCSC) when Isabel paid her a visit in Lewiston. Isabel asked Lucinda if she would like to work for her making baby cradleboards and teaching other Native American crafts to Upward Bound students. "You know, I still don't know how Isabel found me," said Lucinda. "I didn't have a job at the time, so I said yes." When she was a teenager, she had attended Upward Bound for one year at Big Bend Community College in Moses Lake, Washington, so she was familiar with the program.[3]

Lucinda was raised on the Colville Reservation. Her mother, Edith Williams George, was a full-blooded Nez Perce descendant of Chief Joseph's Wallowa band, a group that was exiled to Colville after the 1877 war. She recalled:

> My mother spoke the Nez Perce language fluently and taught me to take pride in my background. She was also a horsewoman and worked to establish the first longhouse for the Umatilla Tribe. She also taught them some of the Nez Perce language. I learned to dance as soon as I could walk. This was not like dancing at powwows. We danced and drummed to keep the people's spirits alive, so they could carry on.
>
> My grandfather, Albert Williams, was what was called a "mush chief," rather than a war chief. He would make sure everyone had food and shelter. If someone passed on, it was his job to make sure orphans were taken care of.

Lucinda learned to make moccasins by watching her great-grandmother as she worked around the woodstove. "My grandmother didn't speak much English, so I learned by simply observing and keeping my little mouth quiet," she added.[4]

Isabel brought beads and elk bones and other raw materials for Native American crafts to the Upward Bound class during the summer of 1975. The students made chokers, horse regalia, necklaces, and, for the expecting mothers, cradleboards. The cradleboard was traditionally used to carry an infant on the mother's back so that her hands were free to work. Lucinda noted, "I instructed her on the proper dimension and shape of the cradleboards, and she had her husband John cut them to size. I think she even paid for the plywood."[5]

Two years later, in 1977, Lucinda went to work for the Idaho State Department of Education's Indian Education department in Lewiston as the first preschool teacher for indigenous students. "When I started to teach, I took Isabel for my role model because she was a very strong woman with a good heart for the people. Isabel was very resourceful and knew a lot about the Indian way of life. She always went to her students' families' funerals and attended the Chief Joseph and Warriors Memorial Powwow in Lapwai. She went to Native American Awareness Week in Lewiston. She seemed to be everywhere."[6]

Lucinda stayed in touch with Isabel even after she went on to work as a police officer, earning the rank of sergeant while working for the Wenatchee (Washington) Police Department from 1980 to 1987. She then returned to school and finished her bachelor's degree in criminal justice before going back into law enforcement for the city of Orofino on the Nez Perce Reservation.

"In 1988, I called Isabel to see if she had a summer position open at Upward Bound. She said 'Yes, hurry up and get your application in.'" Lucinda spent that summer working for Upward Bound as a dormitory counselor and matron for the female students, assisting Isabel in other areas when needed.[7] She added,

> Isabel knew all of the families of her students and the specific students who were struggling the most at that time. Many of them were having issues with their parents. A lot of these kids had what you would today call post-traumatic stress. Whether it was due to historical trauma or the fact that they were from third- and fourth-generation alcoholic families, some of them felt they had no reason to live.
>
> Isabel would do much of what would be called counseling today. She would assure them that they have a life to live and they should stay with us. She would have a meeting with her staff and say, "Okay, so we really have to keep an eye on this one." She did everything she could to help them stay in the program.[8]

Lucinda is retired today from an influential career in law enforcement. Anthropologist Carolyn James documented her story in *Nez Perce Women in Transition, 1877–1990*.[9]

CROSSING THE CULTURAL DIVIDE

Bob Wheaton, now sixty-two, attended Upward Bound from 1973 to 1977. Today, he works in California as a high school teacher and tennis coach. "If you were not white, you were not going to go anywhere in those days," said Bob. "We were basically segregated in the public schools, and there were no expectations for us if we were from the reservation. Isabel provided a support system, which is what many of the kids needed. If it weren't for her, many natives and non-natives would not have gone to college. A lot of her former students are now even becoming elders."[10]

Bob's family is European American, with some Mescalero Apache roots. The Wheatons came to Plummer on the Coeur d'Alene Reservation in the 1960s. Six of eight siblings in his family have college degrees; his brother John, who also attended Upward Bound, is a physician. Bob noted, "The small Upward Bound classes gave me confidence in math and English. There were study skills classes, reading, art, and physical education. Upward Bound is where I first picked up a tennis racket. I played tennis in Plummer on the only paved road in town.

Isabel with the blanket awarded to her by the Nez Perce Tribe in 2006.
Private collection. Photograph by Elinor Michel.

There was nothing there in the way of services at that time. Coming to the University of Idaho back then diminished the fears we had of being on a college campus. If not for the Upward Bound program, the reservations would still be in the dark ages in many ways regarding education."[11]

Bob recalled that the U of I campus in the 1970s lacked ethnic diversity. "During a dance, when we arrived on buses, the local white kids left or would not participate. Native American students were not appreciated because they were considered a threat, or just not understood because of a lack of education. There was a distinct feeling you had of being different when you went there. Living on the rez was safe. There, you did not have to worry about this stuff. The reservation was an imaginary bubble where you felt safe."[12]

Along with the safety of familiar surroundings on the reservation came social problems that tribal communities have been facing for generations, problems that stem from a legacy of conflict and historical trauma. After leaving his hometown, Bob went to a mental health counselor to tell his story: "I told her I knew of twelve people who had committed suicide, and she was shocked. But I thought this was normal."[13] He had plans to become an architect, but after working as an Upward Bound counselor, he decided to pursue a career in education instead. Upward Bound counselors were adults, oftentimes college-age students who worked part-time in the kitchen or teaching classes. For the most part, they had in interest in education, lived in the dormitories, and took on responsibility for student behavior.

Counselors had many tasks. They served as role models and arranged evening activities such as softball, golf, or roller-skating at the local Moscow rink. They assisted students at study table and later in the evening made sure they were in bed with lights out. Counselors also provided personal assistance when needed, such as taking an ill student to the clinic. When a female student arrived at Upward Bound with a baby, one of the counselors even served as a babysitter while the young mother went to her classes. Because they were always around and could provide teachers with additional perspectives on students' situations, they were indispensable to the success of the program.

The counseling experience changed Bob's direction in life. "I decided I would rather work with students and be social than sit there drawing lines for hours and hours. I wanted to help kids," he said. "The Upward Bound program sometimes does not work due to problems like substance abuse, but Isabel gave everyone a chance. For many kids, it can break the cycle of poverty."[14]

After graduating from college, Bob returned to work for Isabel for eight summers as a counselor and science teacher. Thanks in large part to Upward Bound, he completed undergraduate studies at the University of Idaho and earned two master's degrees in California. He worked as a program manager of a tribal school in Seattle before continuing his career as a high school science and history teacher in Washington and California. "Once you get kids involved in education, it becomes a part of their lives, but they must be exposed to it at a young age," he said.[15]

Bob and his siblings were not enrolled tribal members, yet he grew up as part of the Native American community, joining tribal summer camps in the mountains near Sandpoint, where he learned to ride horses. The Wheatons lined up in Plummer with other Indian children to see the dentists and doctors who came to town for medical visits in truck-drawn trailers. "I had all the disadvantages of living on the reservation, with none of the financial benefits of being a registered tribal member," he noted.[16]

Bob observed that Upward Bound served to acculturate native and non-native communities that had long been removed from one another; after the mining industry collapsed in the Silver Valley in the early 1980s, underprivileged non-native students from Kellogg, Wallace, and other towns found themselves side by side with Native American kids who made up the majority in the program. Because of generations-old animosities, these two groups did not always get along. "When we played Mullan [a high school in a white community] at basketball, we would be antagonized from the other side of the gymnasium, but the police always stayed on our side, expecting trouble. When we played other towns, it was sometimes one culture against another. When we played another tribal town, it would be one nation against another. Lapwai had a great football team in the 1970s. We dreaded playing them."[17]

The complex historical landscape of northern Idaho became an important aspect of the Upward Bound curriculum. Lucinda George worked one summer at Upward Bound as a substitute teacher for Bob Wheaton, subbing in his treaties class. "I had them all sit on big pillows, and we would discuss treaties between the tribe and the US government," she said, "including the treaty of 1855, which established the first Nez Perce Reservation. Then they would go to the law library to research details. They would return with interesting homework and reports of their own about our treaty."[18]

After a full week of classes, Isabel and her staff would take the students on weekend rafting trips on the Selway River, to the movies, or to a bowling alley. "These were the fun things that would keep their interest after all the books," said Lucinda. "These were things that their families did not have the connections to do, or the money."[19]

In 1989 Lucinda's son, William Simpson, a student from Lapwai High School, was looking for work. Isabel took a look at his math scores and saw that they were high, so she put him to work as a math tutor. "The next year [Isabel] wrote a grant that established a tutoring program at Lapwai High School, and William went to work there also. As I said, Isabel is very resourceful."[20]

Each year, the program became more effective as Isabel realized that the key to success was structuring time efficiently and holding students accountable. Each student was given a stipend of $7.50 a week for completing their studies and cleaning their rooms, but demerits for bad behavior would lead to reductions in the stipend. "We paid a lot of attention to where the students were and what they were doing. Anyone who was late would have to report to me and attend extra study hall time. Pretty soon they would be waiting at classrooms for teachers to arrive," Isabel recalled. "Many of these kids had always skipped school or were late. A big part of this was about changing habits. If they thought they could come late and not be penalized, they would."[21]

INSPIRATION VS. LIMITATION

Bill Picard was an Upward Bound student who pushed the limits with his teachers. It took some time for Isabel to find the right opportunity to help him turn things around for himself and get serious about his studies. Picard, now sixty-one, was part of a rowdy group of Upward Bound boys who picked Isabel up on their shoulders and started carrying her toward the swimming pool for a dunking. "She yelled out, 'If I hit that water, nobody will get their stipends for the week,' so we all let her back down," he recollected.[22]

Picard is descended from the White Bird band of the Nez Perce. During summers, he worked in the farm fields as a laborer, bucking hay bales and picking rocks. "One day, a teacher advised me to learn the job well, because Indians don't go to college," Picard said. After that, he enrolled in Upward Bound to get his grades high enough to enter college, but at times he got into trouble on the U of I campus. At one crucial point during the summer session, he was called aside by Isabel and given a talking to. "She gave me all the reasons for doing better. No one had ever pushed me before. Isabel and my mother were the only ones who ever inspired me to do better. If it were not for Isabel, I would never have graduated from high school."[23]

Bill Picard and his brother Daniel, an attorney at the Bureau of Indian Affairs (BIA), grew up in the farming community of Craigmont, Idaho, on the Nez Perce Reservation. Both attended Upward Bound. Bill said there has always been more racial prejudice on the reservation than in a city like Boise.

"When my brother left high school, I was the only native student left. I was an easy target for anything that went wrong in town or at school. I still have many lifelong friends from Craigmont, but there was prejudice against my family. We had to work twice as hard." One day during class, one of Picard's high school teachers struck him, an incident that led to a fistfight in the classroom. Police were called to the school. Although witnesses to the incident backed up Picard, saying the teacher hit him first, no charges were brought against the teacher or Picard. "It was like nothing ever happened," he said.[24]

Picard graduated from Lewis-Clark State College and then worked in the education field for twenty years. Since that time, he has worked with state, federal, county, and tribal governments to protect and enhance treaty rights to preserve the Nez Perce way of life.

"Upward Bound not only helped Indian people but also other students in the area who were struggling and lived in poverty. It helps you socially to interact with adults. We went to museums and on rafting trips with kids from many different areas—Hispanic kids, white kids, and black kids. We played softball games in Moscow against the Coeur d'Alenes."[25]

Some years after starting his career in education, Picard ran into the teacher who had told him to keep loading hay bales and give up on the idea of going to college. At the time, Picard was attending an educational conference as a member of the Nez Perce Executive Committee. "He said that I was the last person he ever expected to see at such a conference," recalled Picard.

Now married for thirty-five years, with five children and eight grandchildren, Picard has served on the Nez Perce Tribal Executive Committee for sixteen years. He brings three college degrees—in applied science, liberal arts, and social science—to the task of protecting the general health, welfare, and safety of tribal members and their natural resources. This includes work in preserving indigenous fisheries and hunting rights, and networking with other tribes.

During his Upward Bound summers, however, he tested the patience of Isabel and the other teachers. "Isabel was the first person who ever told me that I was capable of achieving something," said Picard. "Even now, she says I should go get a master's degree. Isabel was more of an auntie than a teacher. I grew up with my cousins, who I called brother and sister. If your mother's sister disciplined you, it was part of the native culture. Isabel was not only the director of Upward Bound at U of I, she was also considered part of our family."[26]

Thanks to Isabel's encouragement, Picard was able to complete the program and go to college. There were some occasions when an Upward Bound student would voluntarily exit the program, and once in a while a student would be sent home for inappropriate behavior, but it didn't happen very often, Isabel noted. Despite the social tensions that sometimes existed in their home communities, issues of race never led to disagreements at Upward Bound. "I can never recall an incident like that between natives and non-natives in all those years," said Isabel. "They enjoyed socializing with one another."[27]

Isabel and her staff went to students' graduations, powwows, and family funeral ceremonies. "If you are going to work for a community, you have to be committed to the things the community thinks are important," she said.[28]

Yet Isabel remains steadfastly practical and unbiased in her approach to accountability and thrift. She understands the importance of saving and planning for the future. "I have always felt that a primary goal is to help kids learn to make a good budget and manage the money that they have. I believe this should be a prerequisite before going to the many food banks around town. There are some people who go to several food banks in the course of a single day. That is dependence, not independence."[29]

In a 2013 letter to the editor of the *Moscow–Pullman Daily News*, Isabel illustrated the difference between giving someone a hand up rather than a handout, how enabling rather than inspiring can keep a person down. "If you are comfortable being disadvantaged, you will remain disadvantaged," she wrote.[30] Isabel's outlook on life was born from struggle and uncertainty. She was a child of the Great Depression and learned young how to take care of her neighbors, a habit that for her family transcended cultural differences.

Chapter 5

LOLA CLYDE

ISABEL BOND'S passion for community service was shaped to a large extent by her mother, Lola Clyde, a schoolteacher and child of the Palouse. Lola's mother, Isabella Gamble, was a highly educated, ardent suffragist and prohibitionist who celebrated the fact that the state of Idaho embraced women's suffrage relatively early. Isabella, the grandmother Isabel was named after, never missed a chance to cast her ballot, traveling from Paradise Ridge to Moscow on at least two occasions each year.

"Almost my first memory of my mother would be of Mama having to leave us to go to town to vote," said Lola Clyde during a series of taped interviews conducted by the Latah County Historical Society. "To see Santa Claus and to vote were the twice-a-year occasions when she just had to go to town. She was very well read, and so I . . . grew up with the feeling that women were equally important to men."[1]

Born in 1900, Lola began to read early, finding in books an escape from the challenges of rural life in Idaho. She attended a country schoolhouse that was frigid in winter. Mud covered the floors during warmer months. "I was fortunate to have good teachers," said Lola. "I'd hurry through the lesson so I could go and get the storybooks and read them; and I soon had them read all through—I'd have to go back and read 'em over again."[2]

IMMORTALITY THROUGH TEACHING

Her earliest ambition was to become the first female University of Idaho graduate to become an attorney. She entered Moscow High School in a class of 110 and graduated in a class of 40, only 12 of whom were boys—the rest having gone off to fight in World War I. Although a bright student, she did not have the financial resources to attend U of I; instead, she attended Albion State Normal School for one year to earn a teaching certificate.

The Albion campus was built in 1893, one of only two teaching colleges in early Idaho. Situated in the town of Albion, its red brick buildings stand mostly empty today in the hills south of Twin Falls in southeastern Idaho. The Albion School had a thriving campus during the 1920s and 1930s, with sports teams called the Teachers. Albion was eventually renamed the Southern Idaho College of Education, graduating more than six thousand teachers before it closed in 1951. Thereafter, Albion's teacher education program was reassigned to Idaho State University in Pocatello.[3]

"You could get a job with one year at normal school, and you could go out to teach, so I settled for that," said Lola. By the time she arrived at her first college classes, she was well versed in literature. "My teacher asked me if I had ever read *David Copperfield.* I said, 'Oh yes, I have. I've read it twenty-five times,' and he was shocked."[4]

Lola's teaching career brought her right back into the rural country schoolhouses in northern Idaho where she first learned to read. She relied largely on instinct and compassion to instill a love of learning in her students. "We didn't have the counseling, we didn't have the time, you know. It was all we could do to get three R's (reading, writing and 'rithmatic) taught and their noses wiped and their hands clean, and their overshoes off and on."[5]

Lola abandoned her plans to study law, choosing instead a career that would inspire in others her own love of learning. "I know that in the rural schools where I taught, many of my big girls went on to become teachers themselves. The reason they gave was that I always told them

Lola (Gamble) Clyde in the mid 1970s. *Courtesy of Latah County Historical Society.*

what fun it was to teach, that this was our immortality. That we dipped our fingers in immortality and it went on and on out into the lives of people."[6]

Young Isabel, a farm girl and tomboy, was also listening. She knew her mother had attended the University of Idaho while continuing to teach at country schools, including the Snow School south of Moscow and the Gray Eagle School, from 1921 to 1922. Despite whatever notions of cultural prejudice may have still existed in Moscow, Lola kept a blind eye to whether her students were white, Native American, or some other ethnicity. "I knew there were some children with black eyes and some with blue, and some were a little quicker in the reading. I always knew that they were going to make a big contribution in the world. I had great respect for all of my children. I was like a mother to them," she said.[7]

THE GREAT DEPRESSION

In 1928, Lola Gamble earned enough credits to graduate from U of I; shortly afterward, she married Earl Clyde, the boy next door, even though his door was some two miles across Paradise Ridge. Earl was an unassuming farmer who had not attended college, but he was an avid reader and learned about farming from his father during an era that went from horses to tractors. Lola and Earl moved to the Clyde farm on Zeitler Road to spend their lives farming the slopes below Paradise Ridge, just as Earl Clyde's father had done.

Within a year, the Great Depression devastated the United States economy. During those challenging times, the four Clyde children were born, one after another. Isabel was scarred forever by the desperation brought on her family during this economic collapse. "We were down to twenty-eight cents, you know, and I had about seventeen hired men to cook for," said Lola. "I didn't have time for regrets or anything else. I was just too busy trying to keep food on the table for everybody."[8]

During the first years of the Clydes' marriage, the Depression sent many farmers into bankruptcy and desperation. They had seen crop prices drop steadily during the 1920s, following the high demand of World War I. The stock market crash of 1929 dealt another blow to an industry already in decline.

In 1932, the year Isabel was born, Lola and Earl, despite owning a vast farm that stretched beneath Paradise Ridge, could not make enough money to feed their family. They waited along with hundreds of others in the bread line in Moscow. "My young husband, myself, four babies all under four years: three hanging onto my apron, one under it," recalled Lola. "Nine hundred acres of surplus wheat to harvest and only broken tools. There was simply too much bread and not enough money."[9]

Lola maintained her family's close ties to church and community across many miles of the rolling Palouse country, which to an outsider can look like a labyrinth of meandering valleys. She continued teaching at Smith School in the Cow Creek area north of Genesee until Depression-era laws were enacted to keep women at home with their families. All the Clyde family could do was hold on for better times.

Then heaven smiled upon them when the International Harvester Company offered to send two experimental combines to cut the crops on the Clyde farm, along with a support crew of engineers, designers, and consultants. During that harvest season, the thermometer read 98 degrees in the shade and climbed to 128 degrees in the house.

One morning at ten minutes to noon, a water boy galloped by on a horse to tell Lola that special guests were arriving for dinner. The guests included Alexander Legge, the president of International Harvester; company founder and board president Harold McCormick; and company vice president Sidney McAllister. These titans of the agriculture industry happened to drop in on Isabel's sister Erlene's second birthday. "They sat down at my oilcloth-covered table and drank spring water from my tomato cans with hammered edges," wrote Lola Clyde in a letter to the company in 1965.[10]

In his youth, Legge started out as a cowboy. By the 1930s, he was a legendary businessman. As a specialist in agricultural equipment, he served on the War Industries Board during World War I and was present at the Paris Peace Conference after the war. Since before the Wall Street Crash of 1929, Legge had been serving on the Federal Farm Board, which distributed a revolving fund of hundreds of millions of dollars to stabilize prices and promote the sale of US farm products.[11]

Lola Clyde was prepared for the visit because she had been keeping up on gossip in Washington, DC, having recently read an account of a chat Legge had with social arbiters Dolly Gann and Alice Roosevelt. With so many truly important issues to discuss, the columnists instead asked Legge to comment on the details of dining room protocol in the nation's capital. "Was he beast, bird, or fish?" quoted Lola. "At formal banquets just where should he be seated? With cabinet members or with senators? Above or below the salt? Just where should he eat?" In reply, Legge quipped, "Well, girls, if it will help you out any, I'll eat in the kitchen."[12]

Having read the article, Lola reminded Legge of his now-famous remark when he showed up at the Clyde farm. She brought him into her kitchen, where he was entertained royally but in a rustic style that was now typical in struggling farm households across America: "Into my widespread table went another leaf: onto the table went three more tomato-can goblets and three chipped plates. I think I must have invented those mix and match 'em style dishes. I opened another jar of home-canned beans and boiled them like mad. We already had an abundance of fried chicken, hot rolls, and cupcakes with twin birthday candles in them."[13]

She rang the dinner bell, and the august company of men sloshed cold water across their faces at the pump outside, dried them on the towels she provided, and filed in. "Tall, smiling, gracious Alexander Legge entered my sweltering kitchen. The youthful sparkle of his kindly blue eyes belied the silvery whiteness of his hair," Lola wrote. "Immediately, the harvest heat and the stove heat were beaten back by this gifted storyteller. We rode the range with him in boyhood. We shivered as we shook the early morning frost from blankets in Colorado's mile-high mountain meadows. We all ate 'sourdough and sow-belly' around his cowboy campfire."[14]

Little Erlene Clyde sat on Legge's lap, soothing his sunburn with damp compresses and combing his hair. The group sang happy birthday to her, blew out the candles, kissed Erlene goodbye, and then departed. After they were gone, Lola discovered a five-dollar bill tucked into one of Erlene's slippers.

Legge passed away the following year, after helping to establish the nonprofit Farm Foundation, with a generous donation to provide nonpartisan policy research and forums relating to agriculture. "The half million dollars Alexander Legge left for agricultural research brought no more happiness than did that five dollars," wrote Lola.[15]

The situation of the Clyde family improved slowly, as did the overall US economy, but Isabel Bond, recalling the financial struggles of her youth, has remained frugal and hardworking all of her life. During the Depression years, a small portion of the lowest end of the Clyde farm was separated off when the new highway was built. Because it was no longer contiguous with the rolling hills above, the federal government compensated the Clyde family for the intrusion and left them with title to the property. A manse that once belonged to a minister in Moscow was relocated to this cut-off portion by the Bond farm many years later and thereafter called "God's Acre." The Bond family carried on this tradition of relocating old houses to their available property, creating rentals and a steady source of income for future generations. One home the family bought for one dollar sits next to Highway 95, just outside Moscow.

LOLA MAKES HER MARK

During the 1950s, Earl Clyde went quietly about his business as a farmer while Lola dove into civic affairs with boundless energy and enthusiasm. Earl was understanding, lenient, and even indulgent. He gave his wife plenty of space to follow her passions. He knew better than to argue with her since she had made a name for herself years before on the U of I debate team. "My husband said he should have known better than marry me because he'd heard me debate, and he might have known that a debate would go on the rest of our lives. He said, 'Lola, you just go and do your thing and I'll do my thing.'"[16]

Soon Lola held seats on the school board, library board, and the local Red Cross board. She later served the Gritman Hospital, the mental health center, and the county health unit. Never a bored farm wife, Lola Clyde at one time was on fourteen different boards for Latah County and the town of Moscow, raising money for everything from schoolbooks to the Idaho Youth Ranch. Lola's legacy of community service had a great influence on her daughter Isabel.

"My mother was always involved in civic affairs," recalled Isabel. "She was instrumental in transforming the county's Poor Farm into a more useful facility. In those days, there were no nursing homes. The Poor Farm began as a home in the country with a garden and cows, where people could take refuge when they were destitute. The people there had duties, like tending to the garden and working with livestock."[17] The Latah County Poor Farm eventually included a nursing home with a swimming pool for the elderly. In later years, the nursing home was given over to the hospital for the cost of one dollar and transformed into the Martin Wellness Center. The facility continues to be managed by the Gritman Medical Center.

Isabel came of age during World War II, when many young men were fighting overseas. Gasoline was scarce, and trips to town were infrequent. Yet her mother found time to attend to any number of civic duties, bringing a light heart to her social responsibilities. "She had not only Christian outreach, but Irish wit and fun to go with it," wrote former Latah County commissioner and Republican state committeewoman Grace Wicks, who remembered Lola Gamble Clyde in a column she wrote for the *Idahonian* (now the *Moscow-Pullman Daily News*) when Lola passed away in 1993. "We talked nearly every day," wrote Wicks. "'Gracie, we need to laugh more,' she'd say every time we giggled at the silliest things either of us could donate to the joy of the day."[18]

Grace Wicks was born on the Nez Perce Reservation. When Lola sent her fresh tomatoes or a box of raspberries, they were often carried by a Native American messenger from her daughter Isabel's Upward Bound program. Lola and her younger sister, Elizabeth Gamble Wahl, would cook for their big brothers, John and Gus Gamble, while they worked the harvest at the Clyde farm. Two other Gamble brothers had sought work elsewhere. "None of these men married, so when it was time for terminal care, some of them came to Lola, who looked after them almost to the end, when the hospital was necessary," wrote Wicks.[19]

UNCLE GUS

If her mother instilled a sense of social obligation in Isabel, it was her uncle, Gustavus A. "Gus" Gamble, a friend of the Nez Perce, who had the greatest impact on how she directed her efforts toward serving indigenous communities. Gus was born in 1891 at the Gamble homestead on Paradise Ridge. As a young man, he farmed "down on the rim" with his brother John, on the rich soil that rests on the flat tops of land bordering the Clearwater River to the north. This land is cut deeply by canyons and reaches from Kendrick to south of Lewiston, including the canyon that extends to Lapwai, where Gus Gamble had many friends. Gus, John, and their hired man, Shorty Hill, loaded heavy wheat sacks onto wagons and trailers, and pulled them behind eight-horse teams to town.[20]

"Gus liked the Indians, and they liked him," said Isabel's first cousin, David Wahl, a retired engineer and farmer living near Genesee. As a young man, Wahl spent a winter at the Gamble farm, remodeling his grandmother Isabella Gamble's house. "There was a Nez Perce trail that ran right through that east end of Paradise Ridge to a traditional camas bulb digging area near the Moscow Cemetery. Moscow was called 'Hog Heaven' many years ago because the pigs loved digging up the camas bulbs there. I can't imagine the Indians were very happy about that, but my grandmother welcomed the visits from the Nez Perce who traveled through."[21]

Wahl has maintained a tradition of reading his Uncle Bert Gamble's poetry at family gatherings. Bert was nicknamed "the Palouse Laureate" for his near-weekly contributions in verse to the *Genesee News*. "I spent time with my Uncle Bert, listening to him read his poems," said Wahl. "One day I woke up with a poem of my own going through my head. When someone passes away in the family, I will bring out the poetry and family histories and share them with everyone."[22]

Wahl's father Tom went to the nearby Gray Eagle School, along with the kids in the Nez Perce Penney family, the same school where Lola Clyde taught before she was married. The Penney family had a farm four miles from the Wahls' place. "There was a time when the Gray Eagle School did not have a name. The story I heard is that one day one of the students, one of the Wardrobe boys, shot a gray eagle and it stretched out wider than his arms were long. From then on, it was named Gray Eagle School," said Wahl.[23]

Wahl has fond memories of his Uncle Gus, who stood six feet tall and was well-muscled from a life of hard work. Gus Gamble met legendary Nez Perce rodeo star Jackson Sundown at Lapwai, where Gus spent time visiting friends and in later years traded fruit and vegetables from the back of his truck. Sundown was a prodigiously skilled horseman and bronc rider who rode into legend among western tribes after winning the World Saddle Bronc Championship at the 1916 Pendleton Round-Up.

"A lot of cattle used to come through here near Genesee, and Uncle Gus would organize rodeos each summer," said Wahl. "He was a bucking bronc rider. So was Jackson Sundown, so the two became friends. Sundown was older than Gus, but he was still riding when Gus was a young man. Gus greatly admired Sundown, and Gus was a pretty good rider himself."[24]

Wahl said the two men visited with one another at rodeos in Lewiston, Genesee, and Pendleton. Jackson Sundown, known as Tolsits to the Nez Perce, a famous all-around cowboy, horseman, and horse breeder. He was also a survivor of the Nez Perce War. According to the Nez Perce National Historic Trail website, Sundown was fourteen years old when the war broke out. A nephew of Chief Joseph, he was entrusted to tend horses while the tribe decamped.[25]

"The story I heard," said Wahl, "is that a US Cavalry officer threw a blanket over him during one of the battles to protect him from harm and later got him to safety."[26] Sundown followed some two hundred warriors into Canada after the Battle of Bear Paw, the final battle of the Nez Perce War, and resided for two years with Lakota Chief Sitting Bull; when he left, he crossed the border into Washington and then Montana, where he married and had two daughters.

Sundown returned to Idaho and in 1912 married Cecelia Wapshela; they lived on her ranch at Jacques Spur, six miles east of Lapwai. By 1914, he became a favorite at rodeos, wearing colorful shirts and tying his braided hair under his chin. Well into his middle years, his presence at a rodeo competition could demoralize bronc riders half his age.

"Sundown worked for the Williams family, which had a farm down in the Genesee area," said Wahl. "Williams was a retired cavalry officer who was married to a Flathead Indian woman."[27]

In 1915, at the age of fifty-two, Sundown placed third at the Pendleton Round-Up. He was coaxed out of retirement the following year by sculptor Alexander Phimister Proctor, who was sculpting Sundown at the time. Proctor paid Sundown's entrance fee to the 1916 rodeo in Pendleton, where he made history. "Rodeo judges were not inclined to give credit to an Indian rider due to prejudice at the time," said Wahl, "but the crowd went crazy at them when they tried to ignore his performance."[28]

Sundown made it to the saddle bronc semifinal round and then rode a horse named Casey Jones to move into the finals with two other cowboys—Rufus Rollen and Bob Hall. Both cowboys had excellent rides, but Sundown could not be beaten. "All Sundown's years as a child in the Wallowas riding, and his career in Montana as a horseman, and his rodeo experience showed that day," according to a 2010 *Oregonian* article by Jamie Francis. "It is said that Sundown became one with the horse. As Angel (his bronc) tried one last attempt at throwing Sundown off, Sundown fanned his hat at the horse,"[29] creating one final flourish. The crowd was ecstatic. Jackson Sundown, Tolsits, was named world champion bronc rider that day and became a legendary folk hero to natives and non-natives alike.

Sundown made his last public appearance in 1917 for Idaho governor Moses Alexander. In 1923, he died of pneumonia and was buried at Slickpoo Mission Cemetery near Jacques Spur. A stone monument placed there to remember him states: "Jackson Sundown rode with Chief Joseph at the age of 14 in 1877. He performed in many rodeos in the Northwest and Canada. In 1916 he won the World's Championship at Pendleton and an ovation never before equaled."[30]

SUNDOWN

Uncle Gus ran cattle nearly eighty of his years.
And he could handle horses that many men would fear.
He started small-town rodeos where he'd watch his ranch-hands
ride.
When Oscar or the Clark Boys did well, he felt a certain pride.
Shorty Hill, as bronc rider, was held in high esteem.

And only Felix Warren was as handy with a team,
But there was just one rider of whom he spoke in awe:
The Nez Perce, Jackson Sundown, was the best he ever saw.

Though Sundown was an older man, Gus knew him rather well.
The way they told their cowboy yarns would enchant you like a
spell.
Uncle Gus threshed wheat at Starbuck when he was twenty-five.
The Roundup at Pendleton would make a young man feel alive.
He could go by stage or horseback and be there on Roundup Day.
The best riders in the world would come to make work into play.
I'm not absolutely certain that he made it there to see.
But told the story as if he'd seen it, just like living history.

Jackson had a work-worn grace about him from riding bareback
as a child.
He knew each move before the horse did: rough and jagged, ever
wild.
The 1916 crowd had seen him ride for many years before.
He was now the favorite, and had the leading score.
It galled the judge's prideful hearts to see an Indian be the best.
In past years they had denied him honor when he'd beaten all the
rest.
But now the crowd had had enough of the judge's stinginess,
They would surely tear the stands down in their unhappiness.

The crowd was getting mighty angry, the judges were un-nerved,
And Jackson Sundown got the honor he deserved.
We made a Sunday pilgrimage, this famous cowboy's grave to
seek.
He rests near Saint Joseph's Mission, within sight of Mission
Creek.
There exists a moving picture from the 1915 rodeo.

It's been combined with stills-in-motion from the 1916 show.
These authentic pictures graced the movie that the Wildbill
family sold,
But I've got Color-Action-Visions from the tales my uncle told.

—David Wahl[31]

One Fourth of July around 1920, Gus, his brother John, and Shorty Hill showed up at the Independence Day celebration in Moscow with a young Nez Perce woman. "It was Prohibition, and the Demon Rum was banished except for here and there," wrote Grace Wicks in 1978. "The girl was to sing for us. Mounted on the faithful family riding horse Ol' Blue, the maiden was gallantly brought before the grandstand and her mount held steady by Gus. Her skirt was a little narrow for astride riding, but no matter, she had the best-looking legs," wrote Wicks.[32]

In a clear soprano, the young woman began to serenade the crowd with this popular ballad:

She's only a bird in a gilded cage,
A beautiful sight to see . . .
Her beauty was sold for an old man's gold,
She's a bird in a gilded cage. . . .

Gus then helped her from the saddle and escorted her to her seat in the grandstand.

Gus had once owned a ranch of his own near Genesee, overlooking the Clearwater River, but he lost it during the Great Depression. When the economy collapsed, crop prices dropped, and he became overextended. He managed to sell his land, but only in time to clear his debts. Thereafter, Gus found work where he could, often living in rented places on the Nez Perce Reservation, where he had many friends, or staying at the Gamble farm for seasonal work.

Gus learned some of the Nez Perce language and attended festivals and powwows. He shared stories about Indian Country with his niece Isabel, giving her and her sister an "Indian pony," which they road across

Paradise Ridge between the Clyde and Gamble farms. Thus began Isabel's lifelong involvement with horses.

Gus brought Nez Perce friends to visit his relatives and spent much time on the reservation, participating in native traditions. While the Christian Nez Perce were gathering at Talmaks for church services and hymns, Gus joined his friends from non-Christian Nez Perce families at Lapwai to play stick games and gamble. "Uncle Gus would bet a silver dollar on the outcome, and at the end of the game an elderly native woman would disperse winnings," said Wahl. "He also went with his Indian friends to rodeos."[33]

Native Americans were allowed free admission to the Chief Joseph Days rodeo in Joseph, Oregon, as long as they agreed to ride in the rodeo parade. One summer, Gus's Nez Perce friends, including Sammy Smith from Kamiah, tried to smuggle him into the rodeo as an Indian, but he was stopped at the gate. The ticket puncher saw through the ruse and began to explain that the white guy would have to pay. "Gus stayed in character and replied in Nez Perce to one of his friends, 'What did he say?' The ticket puncher and his friends were so impressed that he could speak Indian that they let him in for free anyway," said Wahl.[34]

When Gus Gamble died in 1978, Grace Wicks recalled that the Nez Perce Tribe had made him an honorary member. "He lived with them those last years along the Clearwater. For his service there will be as many dark faces as light ones in that gathering, for they held him dear," wrote Wicks. "His niece, Isabel Clyde Bond, heads the Upward Bound program at U of I and shows the understanding of the family for their Nez Perce neighbors. I stopped by this fall one day and Isabel was loading her station wagon for a trip to the valley, and sure enough, there were three very brunette heads among her carful. It was a happy batch of kids off for an adventure. Gus would have approved and most likely have brought a big box of candy to send them on their way."[35]

When Gus stopped farming and took life easier, he had a fruit stand business at the foot of Hatwai Creek. "You could get the best melons in the valley from that stand. You could get them, but most of the time you couldn't pay for them. Gus gave them to everybody he liked and he liked almost everyone he knew," wrote Wicks. "A kindly acquaintance once said 'Gus can chase after you with a gift faster and happier than anybody I know. He was said to be a true son of the Gambles, who gave away more than most folks ever had.'"[36]

Gus was the fourth of the Gamble brothers to go, with Jim the first. His sister Lola canceled a Thanksgiving trip to stay by Gus's bedside during his last hours. Her brother was restless, and toward the end of the day, he kept raising his arm. One of the nurses asked why, and Lola took a long pause and then said, "I think he's driving his team." She then leaned close to his ear and said gently, "Gus, we have put the horses up for the night. They are all safe, fed, and warm in the barn. You can rest now." Gus's arm came down with great weariness, wrote Wicks: "His chores had been done."[37]

LOLA'S LEGACY

Lola worked with the Ladies' Aid Society of the First Presbyterian Church in Moscow, whose members carried out evangelism among families of the church, visiting the sick and bereaved, and helping one another in any way they could. Besides raising money to carry on the work of the church, they held bazaars and suppers, often paying the minister in-kind with a hog at butchering time or sacks of potatoes. They brought special cakes, pies, and other treats to the sick or bereaved.[38]

"You were there to help them and to be a spiritual comforter as well as a physical comforter," said Lola. "You could get in and turn out a washing for the family if the mother was sick. I think the people who did this gained more than the people who received. You felt very grateful for your own good health and for your own good fortune. You wanted to share with somebody else and try to comfort him or her in what they were going through. I think it worked both ways. It was nice to know in sorrow that you were remembered by other people."[39]

Isabel learned about the virtues of community service from her mother, who was honored by her community when she was named

Inland Empire Mother of the Year in 1952 and Idaho State Mother of the Year in 1972.

Lola contributed to the Latah County Historical Society in many ways. She donated her family's historical papers and memorabilia and led school tours to the McConnell Mansion. City councilwoman and noted citizen Linda Pall once had a conversation with Lola about taxation and asked why some people fought against a tax increase, even when it was for a necessary purpose. "Why, paying taxes is actually a privilege!" Lola said. "We support our schools and our local services . . . the parks and all! I can't understand such mean spirits."[40]

And so it was no accident that when *National Geographic* sent a team to scour the Palouse for notable citizens in 1982, they found Lola Clyde.[41] The woman they photographed holding an apple pie in her wheat field had contributed significantly to the history of a region her family had helped pioneer. She was, in fact, well-known enough to contribute to a national newscast in 1987, when the United States and Russia, locked for decades in the Cold War, finally stood together on the brink of accord. CBS newsman Dan Rather interviewed eighty-seven-year-old Lola Clyde on television for her reaction to the event. She replied, in verse, from Rudyard Kipling's "The Ballad of East and West":

> But there is neither East nor West,
> Border nor Breed, nor Birth,
> When two strong men stand face to face,
> Tho' they come from the ends of the earth!

Dan Rather remarked with a smile, "The lady knows her Kipling." [42]

Lola Clyde also knew a great deal about the history of the region she grew up in, having read and listened to many stories over the years. She often told her daughter Isabel's students about the history of the area and how the European immigrants shaped the society in ways that overlooked the much older history and traditions of the Nez Perce, Coeur d'Alene, and other tribes of the region. "Do you know how the Ellenwoods [a Nez Perce family] got their name?" Lola would ask and then explain that the missionary McBeth sisters at Kamiah renamed an entire Nez Perce family after one of the sisters' uncles back in Illinois—a man named Ellenwood.

Isabel would occasionally repeat this story to some of her students to remind them that indigenous culture and languages used to be arbitrarily altered or repressed for the sake of convenience. If a family's name had been replaced, how much else might have been lost to history?

Chapter 6

NEZ PERCE COUNTRY TODAY

ON A Saturday morning in August 2014, Isabel took calls at her house in Moscow from some friends and former students. After hanging up, she unrolled a large, detailed map of the Nez Perce Reservation, much of it checkered with private property sold during the Dawes Act allotment era, when a change in federal law led to reservation lands being apportioned into private parcels, most of which were soon sold and lost forever from tribal ownership.[1] "I only know of one Nez Perce man who farms over there," she said during an interview. "Almost everything is leased out to white farmers."[2]

The Dawes Act or General Allotment Act ended in 1934, after forty-seven years. Much has changed since then.[3] In recent years, the Nez Perce and many other tribes entered into a program that uses funds from a landmark $3.4 billion settlement to buy back fractionalized parcels of land for group ownership by the tribe. The settlement, resulting from a lawsuit brought by Blackfeet tribal member Elouise Cobell against the US government, is an example of how indigenous people are taking back control of their resources and their future.[4]

In 2007, after she left the University of Idaho, Isabel worked for former Upward Bound student Bill Picard as an instructor at the Northwest Indian College in Lapwai. At that time, Bill was the college's site manager. For three semesters, Isabel, then seventy-four years old, drove ninety miles round trip from Moscow to work with another of her former Upward Bound students, Northwest Indian College professor Phillip (Phil) Allen. She took over Phil's human development course on how to become a successful student, which freed him to focus on other priorities, and she taught an elective course on grant writing at Lapwai for two more years.

"Many of us got our start at Upward Bound," said Phil, who first met Isabel when he was sixteen years old. He is a core faculty member teaching English composition, mathematics, and sciences, as well as in-depth courses in Native American history, treaty obligations, and cultural sovereignty.[5]

Now fifty-five, Phil grew up in Lapwai, the administrative center of the Nez Perce Tribe, at a time when the town offered few opportunities for education or recreation. During a lunchtime interview at the Nez Perce Clearwater River Casino and Lodge, Phil noted, "I remember Isabel's Uncle Gus from when I was a kid. He would swap fruit and vegetables in Lapwai from the back of his truck—apples and pears, melons and potatoes, whatever was in season. We all liked him." The casino is only a stone's throw from where Gus Gamble used to sell produce out of the back of his truck near Hatwai Creek.[6]

The swanky casino has an upscale restaurant and meeting rooms. On the walls hang numerous photographs and cultural artifacts that remind visitors they are on Indian land. A big-budget documentary film plays continually on a nearby screen, featuring tribal leaders, historians, hunters, and language teachers engaged in maintaining Nez Perce culture. Old black and white photographs show the Nez Percians, an all-native swing band wearing traditional feathered headdresses; a Nez Perce baseball team from the 1940s; former tribal chairman Richard Halfmoon in suit and tie, sitting beside Josiah Red Wolf, the last survivor of the Nez Perce War. Standing before the entrance to an arcade of slot machines and an elaborate sports bar is a tall bronze statue of Chief Joseph. Nearby is the office of *Ta'c Tito'oqan*, the newspaper that covers stories of significance to the Nez Perce Tribe and surrounding community.

UPWARD BOUND BEARS FRUIT

Phil Allen first heard about Upward Bound from a cousin. "I made good grades and knew from an early age that I was going to attend U of I," Allen said. "My father thought I should join Upward Bound to get familiar with the campus. Isabel is an iconic figure for many of us. If we did not have parents to talk to, she was there for us. She has a way of making you feel as though you can accomplish anything."[7] Over the many years Isabel worked at Upward Bound, she wrote grants that brought many millions of dollars to the University of Idaho. Phil said there is no way to know how many students, both Indian and non-Indian, Isabel helped during her time at Upward Bound and afterward, providing emotional support, room in her house, and sometimes cash to get by. "I'd tell her sometimes, 'You can't save everyone. Some kids are just not cut out for school,' but she would try anyway. Many of these kids came from broken homes or had trouble with the law."[8]

Isabel helped some Upward Bound students find apartments. She helped others buy textbooks. For others, she gave gas money so they could get to campus, found them furniture, or offered them a place to stay while they completed their studies at the University of Idaho. One year, she donated a van to the Northwest Indian College at Lapwai. Many of Isabel's former Upward Bound students enrolled at the college after high school to continue their education. During the 2014 school year, fifty-eight students at Lapwai were working toward two- and four-year degrees, Allen noted. "We have the highest student retention rates of all six Northwest Indian College sites," he added. "In my opinion, education is the way to go. I don't think it is enough for someone to get a seven-dollar-an-hour casino job and say, 'I am happy,' and that's it."[9]

Allen has been developing a cultural sovereignty program curriculum that would provide site-specific knowledge for Nez Perce tribal members, because each of the six tribes represented by the Northwest Indian College's main campus in Bellingham, Washington, has issues pertaining to specific cultural histories and natural environments. "The Lummi [campus] in Bellingham is a coastal institution, whereas everything here in Lapwai is oriented toward the Columbia Plateau and the Nez Perce. We are trying to provide a sense of place for tribal people, but if you have not been brought up in your culture, how can you pass that on?"[10]

Phil Allen hopes to establish an independent college at Lapwai, one that would not be dependent upon federal funding for its existence, perhaps using casino funding for support. "We want to be as autonomous as possible from the federal government," he said. Allen taught at Lewis-Clark State College and at the University of Idaho before returning to Lapwai. "I never had the academic freedom at those colleges that I now enjoy at Lapwai. Many native teachers go to bigger schools that pay more, but I don't want to work at UCLA or elsewhere. I want to teach the Nez Perce in their home community."[11]

A short drive from the casino is the village of Spalding, situated at the confluence of Lapwai Creek and the Clearwater River. This is where the Reverend Henry Spalding and his wife Eliza first established a mission in 1838, endeavoring to bring Christianity to the Nez Perce Tribe. In 1861, the Nez Perce Indian Agency moved to Spalding and remained there until 1904. The missionary site was preserved by the State of Idaho in 1935, and a hotel and other businesses thrived there until 1964, when Watson's General Store closed.[12]

Today, the Spalding area has a large park with old-growth pine trees, several historic buildings, and a unique and historic cemetery. Many Nez Perce graves are marked with extraordinary collections of hats, charms, beads, and other personal artifacts organized into colorful shrines for beloved relatives and friends who have passed away. The gravestones tell stories of veterans, matriarchs, patriarchs, and fishing rights activists.

Towering above the rest of the gravestones at the Spalding Cemetery are those of Henry and Eliza Spalding. Their monument is surrounded by two tiers of iron link chain. The nearby Lapwai Mission historical marker states that this was the site of "the first home, the first school, and the first church in Idaho." Yet, long before the Spaldings arrived, the Nez Perce lived and fished in the area, presumably teaching their children about the affairs of life and building homes to their liking.

CULTURAL RECLAMATION

A sturdy cut-stone bridge, now out of use, reaches up from the edge of the cemetery to roads connecting farms on the east side of Lapwai Canyon. About five miles up the canyon is the town of Lapwai, which means "Place of the Butterflies" in the Nez Perce language. Down at Spalding, thousands of tourists arrive each year to begin explorations of Nez Perce culture and history, disembarking from automobiles and tour buses on a hill above the cemetery at the impressively built Nez Perce Historical National Park headquarters and visitor center. Inside are cultural exhibits, a theater, and a bookstore. For many, this will be the first stop on a journey of over a thousand miles to sites in the park that primarily follow the path of Chief Joseph's Wallowa band as they fought the army in 1877 while trying to reach Sitting Bull's camp in Alberta, Canada.

The 1877 battles are a perennial favorite of tourists, but the real doings of the tribe take place up the road in Lapwai, where a community center, high school, and numerous tribal offices go about the business of maintaining a sovereign nation within mainstream US society. The tribe's complex government employs about a thousand people, half of them Native American, and includes a tribal chairman and executive council that oversee numerous departments, including fisheries, gaming, education, legal and judicial services, social services, natural resources, and wildlife management. Dozens of professional engineers, artists, historians, scientists, and scholars support the tribe, which has an enormous economic impact on the state of Idaho.

Ann McCormack, economic development planner for the tribe, spoke of a study by a University of Idaho economist concerning the tribe's impact on the region. "Perhaps the most interesting fact is how many jobs we create," said McCormack in a 2015 article in the digital daily *Indian Country Today* news platform. "We're in the top three positions continuously the past 10 years for employment in Region 2. The tribe, in 2013, contributed close to $195 million to the state economy including multiplier effects, and we paid almost $10 million in taxes.

People who don't know the tribe can see at what level the tribe is a driver in the community."[13]

In recent years, the Nez Perce Tribe has become the most influential tribe in Idaho, taking part in politics and conservation issues, and steadily recovering from historical traumas, prejudicial legislation, and the health and social problems that stem from generations of conflict and subjugation. Today, traditional hunting, fishing, and gathering practices continue. Those gathering traditional roots and plants from April through August for meals and ceremonies keep their gathering places secret.

Extensive conservation programs aimed at restoring salmon runs are succeeding in areas that have only recently come under tribal ownership. Legal efforts by the tribe's executive committee led to a 2004 US Supreme Court case and settlement with the State of Idaho that provides water and habitat protection for salmon.[14] The tribe's subsequent management policies for this traditional food source have helped restore salmon runs in the Salmon and Clearwater Rivers and led to the recovery of thousands of acres of land lost during the allotment era. The tribe assumed management of wolf reintroduction plans in Idaho in 1995 when the state refused to do so. The *Natural Resources Journal* reported in 1999 that the gray wolf recovery effort in the northern Rocky Mountains was "perhaps the most successful effort to promote the recovery of an endangered species."[15]

Successes such as these stem from the tribe's insistence that the federal government uphold treaty right obligations to the Nez Perce as a sovereign nation. The struggle has not been waged in court only. In 1980, thirty-two Nez Perce armed themselves to face off with state officials over fishing rights guaranteed by treaty.[16] Open fighting was averted, but the state began to take seriously the issue of tribal fishing rights. Today, traditionalists using hemp nets and deer-antler fishing hooks catch salmon at spots where non-Indian anglers are not allowed.

Tourism in northern Idaho has been greatly enhanced by the establishment of the Nez Perce National Historical Park, which was founded in 1965. A museum opened at park headquarters in Spalding in 1983. The extensive park encompasses thirty-eight sites across Idaho, Montana, Oregon, and Washington, including several sites used by Lewis and Clark's Corps of Discovery in 1805 and many more sites significant to the Nez Perce Tribe that focus on the events of 1877. A record-breaking 300,000 people visited the park in 2018,[17] expanding the cultural legacy to people from far beyond the tribe's original homeland.

Of several battle sites commemorated in the park, the Big Hole Battlefield near Wisdom, Montana, is perhaps the most poignant. By the end of a thirty-six-hour siege, almost ninety Nez Perce warriors, elders, women, and children lay dead, as well as thirty-one US soldiers and citizen volunteers. The remaining Nez Perce managed to regroup and push on for hundreds of miles into the fall of that year before Chief Joseph surrendered in the Bear Paw Mountains of northern Montana, only forty miles from Canada.[18]

Ranger Pete Wilson, known affectionately as "Pistol Pete," often mans the front desk at the Nez Perce National Historical Park headquarters and visitors center in Spalding. He, along with many other Nez Perce guides and interpretation specialists, answers questions about the tribe and the history of the park's sites. Last summer, Pete participated in a traditional pipe ceremony at the Big Hole Battlefield during the 138th anniversary of the battle. "There were no ceremonies at these sites when I was a kid," he said.[19]

After beating alcoholism many years ago, Pete built a community sweat lodge on Lapwai Creek and dedicated himself to recovering and celebrating his native traditions. He is reverent and upbeat when describing his tribal history. Many Nez Perce recall family members who died during the 1877 war. Pete mentions Red Heart, one of his ancestors. "Red Heart was taken into custody in 1877, even though he had nothing to do with the conflict," he said.[20]

Pete explains that it took a hundred years for the tribe to return to the 1877 battlefields in Montana to conduct ceremonies for fallen Nez Perce ancestors. He said the tribe returned only after hearing a message from Sioux elders at Fort Belknap near the Bear Paw Mountains: "Two Assiniboine Sioux elders came from Fort Belknap near Bear Paw to tell us something in the late 1970s. They were Jimmy and Edith Earth Boy. They said they could hear the spirits of the horses and women and children dying on the Bear Paw Battlefield."[21]

The Nez Perce then sent delegates to the Bear Paw Battlefield and, the following year, 1977, to the Big Hole Battlefield to hold ceremonies. Nez Perce elder Horace Axtell, who had been chosen by his elders to help resurrect the Nez Perce language and traditions, arrived with others to conduct pipe ceremonies at the battlefields, praying and honoring the ancestors and remembering the pain and despair they endured.

Pete said the tribe now conducts traditional pipe ceremonies for fallen ancestors at eighteen sites in the region. To maintain contact with the Sioux, the Nez Perce Tribe sent a delegation in October 2014 to Little Eagle, on the Standing Rock Indian Reservation in South Dakota. The Sioux returned the visit the following summer with a delegation of fifteen people to attend the Chief Joseph and Warriors Memorial Powwow in Lapwai. "The last thing they did before they left was give me a pipe," said Pete.[22]

In August 2016, Pete used the pipe to conduct a pipe ceremony at the Big Hole Battlefield. Two pipes were packed with tobacco that day, but Wilford Scott lit only one. "Scottie," as he is known, is a retired navy chief petty officer who was discharged in 1972. He then served for thirty-seven years on the Nez Perce Tribal Executive Committee. "The pipe that was left unlit was there to honor Horace Axtell, who was no longer able to make the trip," said Pete. "Some of our elders are not getting around as much anymore, so they have to train another generation to do these ceremonies. The pipe was smoked by everyone, so all were blessed at the ceremony."[23]

That day, through the pipe ceremony and drum circle, Nez Perce veterans and tribal elders remembered and honored all who had fought and died on the battlefield, including those non-Indians involved in the war. The ceremony was accompanied by Michael Penney and the Nez Perce Nation Drum. No photographs were allowed. The Nez Perce

Appaloosa Horse Club held a parade of riders on horseback. One horse carried an empty saddle to commemorate the men, women, and children who died at the Big Hole Battlefield in 1877. All wore traditional regalia. The lead rider wore a war bonnet from Red Heart's band.

Pete said many things have changed since 1877. The ceremony is open to veterans first, but now that includes men and women: "A long time ago, women were not allowed to even touch a pipe or drum. Now we have women drumming groups and women fighting in military conflicts overseas. So now there are both men and women in the pipe circle."[24]

ISABEL REMEMBERS

There have been many changes to the cultural landscape in northern Idaho over the years, but today the Gamble farm near Moscow looks much as it did some seventy years ago, when Isabel rode her Indian pony across Paradise Ridge from her parents' house at the Clyde farm. Old-growth pine trees reach up from a meadow on a hillside that descends to a white two-story house surrounded by porches that overlook a small garden plot along the dirt driveway. Two horses, including one lanky Appaloosa, graze beside the row of vegetables. Isabel's renters—usually students or teachers from the nearby University of Idaho—planted the garden.

"My Uncle John taught me how to milk cows here when I was little, then he gave me a cow of my own," said Isabel as she looked wistfully up the hill toward the Gamble house during a recent visit. Times were tough when she was a kid. "I was born into the teeth of the Great Depression," she said. "The garden was only one of our responsibilities. Then there was haying in summer and fall harvest. There were never any vacations for us. One summer I punched header [kept the header level on hilly terrain] and my brother kept the combine level. I drove a truck as soon as I was fourteen because during the war there were no hired men around to help out."[25]

Isabel and her siblings played in the barn, made forts in the hay, and when they were older, went up the creek on Paradise Ridge to build forts in the forest. Food was scarce, so there were few game animals left in the woods above the farm.

The Gambles built a separate summer kitchen to keep the main house from overheating. No shade trees were planted around the house because tuberculosis was thought to thrive in shaded areas. In order to keep the main house bearable in summer, the Gamble family's meals were cooked outside in the summer kitchen and served in the house. When the Gamble estate was settled in the 1990s,Isabel and her husband John bought the place. For some years, the fields have not been planted. To help satisfy soil conservation goals in the area, the family is subsidized not to grow crops.

Isabel's Uncle Gus worked and lived from time to time at the Gamble farm, bringing Native American friends to visit. One of the first Nez Perce people Isabel met was Pete McCormack, a friendly man her Uncle Gus brought to the farm. "Uncle Gus would speak Nez Perce to us," said Isabel. "One of the first words I learned was *qepsí's*, which means 'no good.' We loved to work for him. It was hard work, but it was fun for us. We shocked hay, hoed potatoes, and herded cows."[26]

By the time Isabel was in high school, she was well-known for her riding abilities, and became rodeo queen one year at the Latah County Fair. Carlton Cummings nominated her for the Lewiston Roundup's royal court, and in 1951 she was chosen to ride as a princess for the Lewiston Roundup. Isabel began her reign while parading down Main Street wearing a bright red shirt and pants and a denim vest. She made friends with fellow royalty members, including Princess Gail Wolverton Foltz and Queen Mary McDonald Mahoney. "It was a very exciting recognition of my interest in horses, but I wasn't real familiar with the process and what was involved," she recalled. "You know, those were hard times and people didn't have much cash, so those opportunities didn't come on the scene at all."[27]

As she turned to leave the Gamble house, Isabel pointed across the road to several large, modern homes with driveways cut into the rounded tops of the facing hillsides. She said the homes often change hands. "New people come here and think they want to live in the country, but they only think that for a while," she said. In recent years, real

Princess Isabel (right) with Lewiston Roundup royalty, 1951.
Private collection of the Bond Family.

estate development has become a lucrative alternative to farming on the outskirts of the university town of Moscow. On the way back to town, Isabel drove past several small subdivisions and a paved bike path, evidence of the burgeoning growth in recent years.

Moscow is as diverse as any college town these days. There are many different churches now, in addition to the Presbyterian church Isabel's grandfather led during the 1880s. College women carry yoga mats while strolling through the downtown farmers market. The city of Moscow surrounds the University of Idaho campus's impressive rows of sorority and fraternity houses, neo-Gothic administration building, athletic fields, greenswards, and academic halls.

Despite owning an abundance of residential real estate, much of it improved with historic buildings the Bond family has relocated from around town, Isabel drives a rattletrap 2002 Subaru on her many errands—the same car she drove thousands of miles in recent years across the Nez Perce and Coeur d'Alene Reservations and the mining towns in between. She lives—at times with renters—in a comfortable

1960s-era home on a tree-lined road in an older neighborhood on a hill in Moscow. Over the years, her house has provided a home away from home for more Upward Bound students than she can remember. Many of them still drop in for visits. Isabel has numerous Native American keepsakes and artworks as well as an extensive library of books about Indian traditions.

Isabel and her high school sweetheart, John Bond, were married in 1954, shortly after they both graduated from the University of Idaho. The couple had four children in four different states over the next six years as John studied geology and worked in the oil industry as a researcher in Washington, Oregon, Oklahoma, and Texas. In August 1968, Isabel and John moved back to Moscow from Midland, Texas, with their children: Daniel, Paula, Maria, and Charles. John began teaching at U of I, where he headed a project that created a detailed geological map of the state.

Isabel, in need of a job, took an entry-level position at Upward Bound. After she became director of the program in 1973, she welcomed students to her home, where she had always encouraged her own children to believe that they could accomplish anything they set their minds to. It was not uncommon for Isabel to take apart a lawnmower that needed fixing or perform other do-it-yourself tasks. She raced snowmobiles and continued to ride horses well into her senior years.

Upward Bound recalls brought its students together during the fall and spring of the regular school year to keep them focused on their studies and interested in returning to the program the following summer. The girls would stay at "The Bond Shelter," while the boys stayed in the dorms on campus. Isabel's own kids joined Upward Bound groups on summer camping or rafting trips and got to know some of the students who stayed at their house during recalls.

Isabel followed up with Upward Bound students during the school year, consulting with their counselors at the various high schools. She took joy in seeing her students realize their dreams even while she instilled in them a work ethic and sense of accountability, and she became part of an extended, indelible web of relationships that spread across the reservation. Occasionally, Isabel struggled with program administrators and others who tried to veer away from what she saw as Upward Bound's original mission. They called for changes that would have excluded the very students she thought the program was designed to help.

Darlene Dyer recalled the day that Isabel came home from a regional Upward Bound conference upset about what she had heard from a fellow director. "Someone had told the group that he would not accept any students with less than a 3.2 grade point average," Dyer said. "Isabel disagreed with him entirely. She said that's not what the program was designed for and that the whole point of the program was to help underprivileged and at-risk kids, not those who were already doing well."[28]

Chapter 7

⟐ UPWARD BOUND COMES OF AGE ⟐

THE UNIVERSITY of Idaho campus, with its tree-lined Hello Walk, towering fortress-like administration building, and well-appointed dormitories, is rich with symbols of the wider world, its powerful institutions, and complicated histories. The aura of the campus has transformed many Upward Bound students, giving them a new understanding of their potential. With the help of professional educators and student teachers, Upward Bound evolved quickly from loosely based summer classes into a more rigorously structured program designed to hone study skills and open students' eyes to the exciting possibilities of higher education.

In the 1970s, Elinor Michel, a U of I education department faculty member, brought a study skills focus to Upward Bound that she had developed for Chicanos, blacks, and low-income whites while teaching at an Education Professions Development Act-sponsored summer institute run by the University of Michigan in Flint.

"The goal was to build study skills around students' interests," said Elinor, now emerita professor of U of I's College of Education. "We had them create picture collages about their lives and then write narratives around them. We also taught kids how to approach learning, how to plan study time, review notes, and take tests using content that interested them."[1]

STUDY SKILLS AND HANDS-ON LEARNING

Elinor adapted Dr. Walter Pauk's note-taking methods from the Cornell University Learning Center to Upward Bound purposes. The Cornell method involves separating a page of notes into three parts; two-thirds of the page is used for a steady stream of notes, one-third of the page is filled with personal cues, diagrams, topics, and questions to be answered later. The bottom of the page is used to summarize the main ideas. This method allows for easier reviewing of notes and more critical thinking about the material, but the process of learning how to learn was a difficult first step for many Upward Bound students.

"They nicknamed the class 'study kills,'" said Elinor, who taught a mixture of Nez Perce and Coeur d'Alene students and a few non-Indians. "It was an eye-opener for everyone. They learned a lot about one another. I think there had been a lot of misconceptions about Native Americans, what kind of life they lived, how much of a community they have, and how much they cared about one another. Natives are much more willing to help one another out. Most of the rest of us are individuals and look out mostly for ourselves. We are a much more competitive society in terms of general living. Mainstream American society is just more individualistic. After all, that is what the capitalist system is all about."[2]

In 1972, about sixty students and a dozen staff members drove to the Oregon State University Marine Sciences Center on the Pacific Coast. For most of the students, it was the first time they had seen the ocean. Bud Langdon, the Upward Bound director at the time, wanted them to stay in motels, but the students said they wanted to be on the beach, smelling the smells and hearing the sounds of birds. They camped out under the stars at the beach on Saturday night and applied their "study kills" to the science content at the Marine Sciences Center.

Isabel's husband John gave lectures in the study skills class for another field trip along the Columbia Plateau. He explained how weather and geologic forces combined over millions of years to create the colonnade and pillow formations of rocks visible from the highway.

Dan Davis, Upward Bound science teacher, discussing animal furs in study skills class. *From the 1992 Upward Bound yearbook. Photograph by Darlene Dyer.*

Another field trip took students to the planetarium at WSU. When they returned to the University of Idaho campus, they created cardboard planetariums of their own, with pinprick holes to mark constellations. A group of Upward Bound science teachers then had students build two- and three-stage rockets that were set off from ground zero at Guy Wicks Field on campus.

Elinor Michel caught mice in a field near the duplex where she lived and donated them to science. They were used as dissection specimens for the Upward Bound biology classes. At the end of each summer program, a powwow was held on campus, and families of Upward Bound students would gather with townspeople and other students and faculty who happened to be on campus for summer sessions. During this "last day" celebration, families arrived on campus to see what their children had accomplished. At the powwow, the biology students proudly displayed their neatly dissected mice on wooden boards.

In the study skills class, Elinor introduced students to underlining techniques and critical thinking. She led them through the process of writing essays of comparison and contrast. Later, through the Bridge program, Upward Bound's college-bound seniors were given a taste of what college would be like. Because Elinor also taught composition classes at the college level, all of the Bridge students entering U of I took Elinor's college writing classes the following fall, providing them with a familiar face and safe environment. "A lot of Upward Bound students may not have graduated from college, but I believe they all came away with a value for education," said Elinor. "Even though they may not have earned degrees, many of their children went on to do so."[3]

FOSTERING STUDENT ENGAGEMENT

Teachers Darlene (Matson) Dyer and Gail Jensen scrambled during the regular school year to find engaging material to share with Upward Bound students the following summer. "Many of the Upward Bound students came to high school with elementary reading and writing skills, so we shopped for books that were easier to read to get them on board," said Darlene.[4]

One summer, she brought the Upward Bound students copies of *The Jim Thorpe Story: America's Greatest Athlete*, by Gene Schoor, a story about the Sak and Fox Nation member who has been described as the greatest athlete of the twentieth century. She borrowed copies of the book from Wood River Junior High School in Hailey, where she taught during the year, knowing the book would offer a realistic view of overcoming the challenges faced by Native Americans in the arena of sports. "For me, working at Upward Bound was like hands-on professional development because we designed our curriculum to meet the needs of our kids, and we had the federal dollars and college campus resources at our fingertips to pull it off," Darlene said.[5]

For one class, this meant crime-solving using only a jukebox. One student, appointed sheriff, asked questions about a crime. The rest of the class could only respond using the titles of songs from the jukebox. Because music and pop stars were already competing with standard reading materials for students' attention, this approach proved successful. Sports also had the power to bring a diverse group of students together.

In 1985, the Chicago Bears football team produced the "Super Bowl Shuffle," a rap song recorded by team players that became an instant TV phenomenon. The students rewrote the lyrics to the song as the "Upward Bound Shuffle," about their own lives and one another.

During years when the Olympic games were televised, students kept up with the careers of their favorite athletes, so the teachers had them read *Sports Illustrated* articles about how the athletes prepared, where they came from, and what they had accomplished. Then the students were required to create imaginary sports of their own and design training methods and goals for their sports. "They wrote articles about 'grass surfers,' 'hall runners,' and 'egg tossers,'" said Gail.[6]

Throughout these years, Upward Bound students learned about one another's backgrounds in a process of acculturation that had never before taken place on the University of Idaho campus. One of Gail's students, Robert Seward, styled himself as an elite speed reader. He delivered a fictional report on how he planned to train for the 1984 Olympic Games.

Robert's family had moved from Temple, Texas, to the mining town of Wallace, Idaho, when Robert was in eighth grade, just in time for the Bunker Hill silver mine closure. The oldest of five children, Robert watched as his parents struggled to survive in a town with no jobs and few prospects for the future. "We arrived just before the local economy collapsed," said Robert, now fifty-four and working at a Hastings retail store in Moscow. "Wallace was a mining town. The running joke was that the whorehouses paid for the school band uniforms. My father never really had a steady job after the mine closed. I did some babysitting to make money. There were no movie houses, so for three years we never saw one. There were VCR players, but my family could not afford a $1,000 VCR."[7]

Robert's friend, Randy Fink, first told him about Upward Bound, but by the time he could take advantage of the program, Robert was poised to graduate at the bottom of his class. "There was a considerable amount of bullying going on at Wallace High School. The school district simply did not care," he said. Robert was recruited into Upward Bound after being held back from graduating with his class. "I was one of the oldest," he recalled. "They told us to bring clothing, an alarm clock, and not too much money."[8]

Robert was assigned a dorm room at Targhee Hall on campus. He joined the group at orientation and was tested along with the other students for proficiency in math, English, and science. The students were then sorted into four morning classes and two afternoon classes. For Robert, the thriving and diverse town of Moscow was a far cry from the isolated town of Wallace. "It almost felt like civilization again. I can remember the movies that were playing in the theater when I got there–*Ghost Busters* and *The Karate Kid*. There was freedom after classes. We could go swimming at the pool on campus or go into town. Isabel gave me a ride to the Baptist Church on Wednesday nights. I spent a lot of time running around the library, pulling out microfilms of old newspapers or looking up obscure books."[9]

Robert attended dances and health lectures, went on camping trips, and had his first exposure to Native American culture. He was introduced to the history of forced assimilation of indigenous children in boarding schools such as at Carlisle Indian Industrial School, in Pennsylvania, which Jim Thorpe attended, during a time when the US government sponsored the eradication of native traditions and a thorough assimilation of indigenous people into European American society.

"I had only ever been around one or two Indians before and had learned in fourth grade about the Trail of Tears of the Cherokee to Oklahoma, but now the majority of the students around me were native, not only Nez Perce and Coeur d'Alene, but also Apache, Spokane, and one guy who was Crow," recalled Robert. "On one of our camping trips to the Nez Perce Reservation, I ate buffalo for the first time." He made several attempts to complete a college degree before entering the University of Idaho in 1992 at age twenty-six. Isabel encouraged him to attend the Bridge program in order to prepare for college. He then took advantage of Student Support Services and in 1992 was diagnosed with cerebral palsy. "Everyone had thought I was just blind as a bat and uncoordinated," he said.[10]

Shelly (Hall) Smede, student teacher, and Darlene Dyer, teacher, 1993.
Private collection of D. Dyer. Photograph by Isabel Bond.

While studying foreign languages, he worked full-time at a restaurant, as an apartment manager, and at the U of I foreign language laboratory. He eventually graduated with a 2.74 grade point average. Robert then went to work for Isabel at Upward Bound, maintaining a database, writing a monthly newsletter, and attending to numerous other administrative duties. "Isabel could be a sweetheart or a martinet," said Robert. "She put herself in a situation where she worked twelve-hour days, and she expected everyone else around her to have the same amount of devotion. Nobody worked harder than she did, but she was a very demanding boss."[11]

Robert said that new Upward Bound teachers were surprised at the reactions indigenous students had to certain historical contexts. One day, an overhead projector displayed the image of an Indian scout wearing a blue US Army uniform, as was the case when Native Americans allied with US forces against other tribes. "The native kids in the class started booing and hissing, and yelling, 'Traitor, traitor,'" recalled Robert.[12]

At other times, students responded to cultural cues that some teachers didn't recognize at all. Of Athabascan descent, Glenn Williams was born in Los Angeles and raised in Tacoma, Washington, before moving to Lewiston. His first year at Upward Bound, he arrived on campus wearing an insignia that brought respect from fellow students. "I wore a jacket that showed I had worked at BJ's Bingo in Fife, Washington, where many millions of dollars had been won. A lot of the native students were impressed by this," said Glenn.[13]

In 1982, Glenn dropped off his younger sister and brother at Upward Bound. While they pursued their studies and later attended college, Glenn took a job as cook for the Upward Bound summer sessions. He worked for Isabel for sixteen years as food services director and dorm counselor. He recalled that there were a lot of first kisses and first loves on campus during those summers, but it was very sad when the young lovers broke up. "I think a hundred kids must have cried on my shoulder," said Glenn. "I remember a kid breaking down one day, crying. He kept asking why his father had abandoned him."[14]

Glenn said it was not uncommon for Upward Bound students to be caught climbing on U of I buildings because they came from towns where they had never seen a roof that high and were curious. One summer, a young white boy arrived wearing rags and appearing malnourished. "He had been abandoned by his parents and was living with his aunt," said Glenn. "He was so poor, his clothes were almost falling off of him. The Upward Bound teachers all got together and pitched in and bought some clothes for him. He was happy to later join the Job Corps to learn a trade or get his GED diploma."[15]

On several occasions, Glenn joined Isabel on recruiting trips to the Silver Valley or when attending a reservation funeral. In some of the white towns, they would see Nazi swastikas and Confederate flags hanging in the windows. "I wasn't sure if it was safe to get out of the car," said Glenn. "But when we went to a funeral on the Coeur d'Alene

Reservation, it was amazing how many people knew Isabel and me from Upward Bound. They were all like our family."[16]

Glenn knew one young Upward Bound student who dreamed of becoming a police officer. A few years later, he ran into the young man at a service station, wearing a uniform and driving a squad car. He had succeeded in becoming a state patrolman.

Glenn's last five years of working for Isabel were in the Northwest Nations Upward Bound program she established. The program served not only Nez Perce and Coeur d'Alene, but also kids from the Spokane, Colville, Yakama, Umatilla, Shoshone-Bannock, and Shoshone-Paiute tribes. "A lot of these tribes recalled their old historical differences and would shout at one another that they were still going to come and fight them and take their women," he said.[17]

Some differences between students were resolved under the radar, without parental oversight. A case in point is Ollicutt Joseph "O.J." Watters, age forty-five, who grew up in Lapwai and attended Upward Bound each summer while he was in high school.

When O.J. was a kid, Lapwai had no boys' and girls' clubs or other after-school programs for children. In grade school, O.J. joined his father, Irvin Watters, and his uncles in the Spalding Drum, a group that traveled to powwows in Boise, Portland, and elsewhere. During high school, he traveled on Thursdays and Fridays, meeting people from many other tribes. He worked with his father during the summer, bucking hay bales and mending fences. They had a small herd of horses. When he was old enough, O.J. drove to Juliaetta from Lapwai to split kindling for his grandmother to burn in the woodstove she used for cooking and heating her home.

"I tried not to miss more than eight days at school, since that was the limit in the high school handbook," O.J. said, "but in high school I did not have good grades, so I went to Upward Bound to get my grades back up. Upward Bound did well for people. It helped us to understand one another and further our education. It helped to improve our minds. My Aunt Mari Watters worked there for many years."[18]

While on campus one summer, O.J. found himself caught up in a dispute over a young woman's reputation. He learned that two boys had had a scuffle over some unflattering comments made about a girl they both knew. O.J. saw that the trouble would escalate unless something was done about it, and quickly. "The problem was that a fight was likely to break out, everyone would get in trouble, and some of us would get thrown out," said O.J. In an attempt to resolve the issue, he arranged a fight between the two boys in the basement of Targhee Hall.

"I guess you could say I was the culprit," said O.J. "We had spotters at each entrance to make sure no counselors knew what we were doing. It was very late at night. Well, then someone asked, 'Can we make bets?'" Pretty soon, boys were laying down bills on a bench to stake bets on their favorite opponent. O.J. oversaw the fight and spelled out strict rules for no scratching or other fighting techniques that would result in noticeable injuries. Perhaps because of his role in the operation, O.J.'s nickname in the 1988 Upward Bound yearbook was "Sergeant at Arms."

CULTURAL TRADITIONS IN A LARGER CONTEXT

Female students typically showed more interest in academic achievement, Darlene Dyer noted. The girls at Upward Bound were usually better at reading than the boys, so the teachers chose titles and subjects designed to capture the boys' interest. An effective book was *Deathwatch*, by Robb White, about a young boy who, to make extra cash, takes a rich man into the desert to hunt bighorn sheep. The rich man accidentally shoots an old miner and wants to cover it up. The morality tale takes a turn when the boy refuses to conceal the crime and for that he too becomes hunted by the rich man. The students also read *When Legends Die*, by Hal Borland, about an Indian rodeo cowboy who realizes that only by going back to his indigenous roots can he be happy.

Western and Nez Perce stories were read along with stories from classic European literature. Teachers hoped the juxtaposition would allow Native American students to see the similarities between their

Upward Bound students rafting on the Selway River, 1993.
Private collection. Photograph by Darlene Dyer.

own stories and those of other times and places. One summer, they read *Beowulf, A New Telling*, by Robert Nye, a shortened, early reader's version of an epic Old English poem about a hero who faces the menacing monster Grendel, which terrorizes a Scandinavian village, eating its people at night. Gail Jensen spent a week during study skills classes that summer learning and teaching Nez Perce mythology. She knew *Beowulf* would resonate with a living myth in Nez Perce culture that tells of the tribe's creation from the blood of a monster.

Creation stories in Indian Country often form the foundation of ancestral meaning for a particular culture group. The Nez Perce creation story tells of a gigantic monster that lived in the valley around Kamiah and ate all of the animals. Coyote, the Trickster, fooled the monster into swallowing him. Once inside, he used stone knives to cut the monster apart from the inside and release the animals trapped inside. According to local tradition, when Coyote emerged from the remains of the monster, he cut it up and threw the pieces all over the land, creating the Indian people who now inhabit the region, including the Blackfeet, Crows, and Flatheads. Coyote then washed the blood of the monster off his hands. Those drops of blood became the Nez Perce.

The Beowulf tale from eighth-century Europe describes a monster named Grendel that is eventually slain by Beowulf, the king of the Geats. According to legend, a stone hill marking Beowulf's grave can be seen from the sea. The Nez Perce have a stone landmark of their own. Deep within Nez Perce territory, on the banks of the Clearwater River in Kamiah, a curious mound of basalt rock exists on flat ground beside the highway. It is known as the"Heart of the Monster" or just "The Heart" because, as legend has it, this is where Coyote left the heart and washed his hands of the monster's blood, which created the Nez Perce. "The Heart" is one of many ancient sites in the area and a regular stop during Upward Bound field trips. Reading *Beowulf* and the Nez Perce creation story together encouraged Upward Bound students to consider their own traditions within the context of other literary and mythological traditions from around the world.

CREATIVE TEACHING TECHNIQUES

Upward Bound summer sessions began with an orientation for teachers and staff during which Isabel would describe each student's background and particular challenges. Teachers spent a good portion of the week planning lessons that addressed those needs and challenges. "Some of the kids came from troubling, even dangerous circumstances," said Darlene. "Some students came to us as wards of the state for having been in trouble for juvenile crimes. Despite their 'raps,' we found them sweet, cooperative, and not at all criminal. But I always kept these challenges in mind as I designed my lessons."[19]

Darlene said Isabel was eager to support Upward Bound staff in whatever way she could to help them keep students interested in academics. "She had an infectiously positive attitude toward the students," noted Darlene. "One of the most important things Isabel taught me, something that I have practiced for my entire teaching career, is the value of positive communications between students and parents."[20]

During the third or fourth week of the program, after teachers had a chance to really get to know their students, Isabel required each of the ten or so teachers to choose several students about whom they would write letters of appreciation to send home to parents. Darlene recalled, "We would write about admirable characteristics or behaviors that demonstrated each student's success at Upward Bound. We worked together as a staff to make sure that every parent of an Upward Bound student received a letter praising anything from academic success to personal charm. When students found out about 'their letters,' they became eager to live up to this positive image even more or try harder at their studies. I adopted this practice and used it for many years as a public school teacher. It has unfailingly motivated my students and enriched my teaching experience."[21]

Isabel noted that Darlene created a genuine enthusiasm for the kids to engage in Upward Bound opportunities and activities. "She was the one who taught study skills first thing in the morning," said Isabel. "Sixty students would be waiting for her to show up in the morning, even though many of them were known for being late or not showing up at all to class. I think it was because Darlene was very clear about what she expected of them. Many of these students had simply been overlooked in high school."[22]

Darlene and Gail, who was a drama teacher, teamed up to perform a skit that would illustrate to students the need for focus during study periods. Darlene created a character named Denise Dontwanna, who had a hard time completing assignments due to laziness or distractions. Gail would improvise the part of Denise for the students, acting out her bad habits and compulsions to talk on the telephone, listen to music, or eat—anything other than study. "Gail was hysterically funny at acting the part of Denise Dontwanna," said Darlene. "She played a girl who could get nothing done due to constant distractions and interruptions. For this five-minute dramatization, we needed a few props—a chair and table, telephone, boom box, television, and refrigerator. I could easily round up the first few, but the refrigerator posed a problem."

The study skills class met every morning at eight o'clock in a large lecture hall on campus that seated about one hundred people in tiered rows so that a speaker at the front could be seen clearly by everyone. On a typical day, Darlene would stand beside an overhead projector in front of sixty-five students and their teachers and give a fifteen- to twenty-minute lesson or presentation. "I arrived that morning of our first performance of Denise Dontwanna and, lo and behold, there was Isabel's husband John and son Charles hefting a full-sized refrigerator down twenty rows to the bottom of the lecture hall," Darlene said with a smile. "They had no doubt yanked it from one of their rental apartments and trucked it to campus for our short presentation."

ONE STUDENT'S JOURNEY

Some students found their way to Upward Bound through a circuitous route. Brad Filkins was an academically successful Native American student who arrived at Upward Bound during the early 1970s after enduring a challenging semester at Fort Sill Indian School in Oklahoma. His mother, Elizabeth (Halfmoon) Skanen was a full-blooded member of the Coeur d'Alene Tribe. His biological father was a non-Indian forester from Minnesota who took his family to various reservations during a career working for the BIA. "We were never around long enough to get involved in tribal politics," said Brad, who was exposed to life on several Northwest reservations, along with his brother Steve and sister Mary.[23]

Brad's mother divorced and later remarried Hillary "Skip" Skanen, who served as chairman of the Coeur d'Alene Tribe and executive director of the Affiliated Tribes of Northwest Indians. All three of the Filkins children attended Upward Bound. They were taught to value education, but the two brothers also liked to tussle. The fights increased after Brad's mother divorced and moved her family to Pullman, Washington, where she worked as a recruiter for Washington State University. Brad's uncle, Ronald Halfmoon, also worked at WSU.

"In our household, we grew up with a dictionary in the common room. If someone said something I didn't understand, someone would point to the dictionary for me to look up the word. It would be up to me to find out what it meant," said Brad.[24] With his relatively fair skin and Anglo features, Brad takes after his father more than his mother, a fact that brought challenges during his freshman year in high school. In part to separate the two rowdy brothers, Brad was sent to Fort Sill Indian School in Oklahoma when he was fourteen.

The school was situated about two miles from the Fort Sill army installation, the only active army base of all the forts that were built on the Southern Plains during the Indian Wars. Students at Fort Sill Indian School who knew their history understood that the garrison had been established to quell indigenous uprisings in Texas and Kansas. Many knew about Comanche chief Quanah Parker's surrender there in 1875 and about the grave of the great Apache chief, Geronimo, nearby. "Fort Sill was the hardcase school for everybody who had been kicked out of somewhere else," said Brad. "It was a real eye-opening experience for me. The place felt more like a detention center than a school. There were eighteen-year-old freshmen. I felt like a genius down there."[25]

Fort Sill Indian School is closed today. Before World War II, its student body was made up largely of Indians from western Oklahoma, including the Comanche, Apache, Caddo, Kiowa, Delaware, and Wichita tribes. After World War II, many Navajos from New Mexico and Arizona were admitted. By the time Brad Filkins arrived, the school had a diverse mix of tribes from across the nation. Upon his arrival at the airport, a very dark-skinned, very large Oklahoma Indian was there to help carry his bags. The two talked on the way to campus and, luckily, got along well.

"This was fortuitous for me," recalled Brad, "because the next day on campus, another big guy with dark skin saw me having a smoke and grabbed me and lifted me up against a wall. He said I had to give him my cigarettes. I knew I had to fight him and that I would probably get my ass kicked. Well, about this time, my new friend, the big three-hundred-pound student, came around the corner and took this guy and lifted him up and shook him with one hand. He said, 'This is my friend,' so the guy dropped me, and then my friend dropped him."[26]

Brad no longer had to worry about being jacked up for his cigarettes. He made friends with others who were also ostracized because they were either light-skinned or good learners. He was allowed to leave Fort Sill after one semester, returning to his family on the Coeur d'Alene Reservation in DeSmet, Idaho. He attended the Upward Bound program at U of I during the summers of 1973 through 1975. Each fall, he went to Chemawa Indian School in Salem, Oregon, a boarding school run by the BIA.

"Chemawa was a much better school than Fort Sill," said Brad. "Going to Upward Bound each summer gave me a running start into each new school year. It was also a place where I could make new friends." Brad's Tulalip roommate was taking a remedial English course, so Brad would throw words at him that he did not understand, playing the game he learned at home when he was a kid. "By the end of the school year, his reading ability had improved to a college freshman's level," said Brad, adding, "The Upward Bound dorm counselors and staff took good care of us during those summers. Isabel was always encouraging. She told me how to use Upward Bound to prepare for the next year at Chemawa. She also helped me to align my plans for college."[27]

Through Upward Bound, Brad got to know a college athlete and physical education instructor who taught him about weight training and flexibility. "I learned so much that I had never heard before, stuff that I use to this day. The guy was a jock himself. He sat there and talked to us about using high-weight, low-repetitions to bulk up, or vice-versa for endurance and strength. Most of the staff were college students and talked *to* us, instead of *at* us. These were not cookie cutter classes like at Chemawa, where you either kept up or were left behind. We all moved forward together, and I really liked that. If I had questions, an Upward Bound instructor would not shut me down. They would answer us and took individual time with us. It was nice to be treated respectfully and as an individual."[28]

Each year, the Native American students at Upward Bound went to powwows at WSU in Pullman and U of I in Moscow. One year, they were surprised to learn that Olga Korbut, the famous Russian gymnast, was in town and wanted to meet some real cowboys and Indians. There was a parade in Moscow that summer honoring Korbut, and the Upward Bounders who had regalia planned to participate. Having taken up black-and-white photography after his mother bought him a Pentax 35mm camera in sixth grade, Brad Filkins took advantage of the photography classes offered by Upward Bound. At the parade in Moscow that year, all of the Native Americans who had regalia participated in the parade and had a mini powwow for the gymnast while Brad took pictures. Olga Korbut watched the dancers while Brad's brother Steve talked to her through an interpreter.

Brad later attended the Presidential Classroom for Young Americans, a nonprofit organization that gathers students in Washington, DC, for an in-depth six-week study of the US government. "I believe that it was because of Upward Bound that I was selected for this honor," he said.[29] Brad went on to earn a bachelor's degree in science, engineering, and technology from DeVry University. His most recent job post was at Cayuse Technologies in Pendleton, Oregon, a business owned by the Confederated Tribes of the Umatilla Reservation. His brother Steve studied criminal justice before taking a job as a policeman for the Coeur d'Alene, Umatilla, and Tulalip Tribes for twenty years.

Six years ago, Brad's parents, Hillary Joseph Skanen and Elizabeth

Upward Bound students at Wolf Haven, Tenino, Washington, 1993. *Private collection. Photograph by Darlene Dyer.*

Constance Skanen, died on the same day within hours of one another, after spending many years together as husband and wife. "Isabel came to the funeral," said Brad. "She heard about it somehow and came to DeSmet for the service and also made sure she talked to all of us kids. I knew her right away when I saw her. It was very comforting to know that she was there."[30]

EXPANDING STUDENT HORIZONS

Teachers never know the full impact they have on the lives of their students. The Upward Bound experience expanded horizons because Isabel and her staff spent considerable time organizing educational field trips each summer. The students were introduced to theater and other performing arts. They went to Ashland, Oregon, where the works of William Shakespeare had become an integral part of the college town's thespian history, and to Crater Lake National Park. The staff availed themselves of whatever connections or research materials they could gather from college professors on the University of Idaho campus. One weekend, the group went to the nearby seven-hundred-foot-tall Dworshak Dam and Reservoir, touring the fish hatchery complex there.

In later years, U of I Upward Bounders joined other students from around the country at the Space Academy in Huntsville, Alabama, sleeping in "space-pod" bunks after learning about the wonders of astrophysics and off-world travel. In Moscow, they played rounds of golf after classes on the University of Idaho Golf Course. Darlene Dyer joined them, wearing a bicycle helmet just in case a stray golf ball headed her way. "What I came to love about Upward Bound was that we really got to know our students," she said. "We had meals with them, walked them home, or engaged in friendly talks while we were on campus. And we spent weekends together recreating with them or providing some educational enrichment. None of this would ever happen in a public school system."[31]

By the early 1990s, the Nez Perce Tribe was working to help reintroduce the gray wolf to the Northern Rocky Mountains from Canada. Because the tribe had jurisdictional authority over its own land, wildlife biologists behind the reintroduction program found a welcome on tribal lands. In recognition of the role the Nez Perce Tribe was playing in the wolf reintroduction program, the 1993 Upward Bound summer theme was designated as "The Wolf." Darlene found some biologists on campus who were working on the reintroduction program. "Pretty soon our students were wearing wildlife radio-tracking collars borrowed from the biology department, to study the technology" said Darlene. "They used the collars to track one another around campus."[32]

Almost every summer, Darlene and Isabel took a group of students on a weekend rafting trip to Selway Falls. The water below the falls roiled and pushed the rafts swiftly along, but as the river flowed onward, it grew calmer and smoother until the students eventually had to paddle to get downstream and back to camp in time for dinner. One afternoon, a group of students got lazy and just snoozed in the rafts in the sun, despite admonitions from staff to keep paddling. Having already reached the takeout downstream with another group, Darlene and Isabel watched from a bridge over the river as the lazy rafters drifted about, oblivious to the warnings that they were running late for supper.

Darlene recalled an incident from earlier in her Upward Bound career when a group of students decided to have some fun at her expense using water balloons. Well, what goes around comes around, she thought, hatching a plan with Isabel. They went down to the river's edge, giggling like schoolgirls as they filled two buckets with water and then walked back up to the bridge to wait. The kids on the rafts could not escape the cold water that fell from above, and they all laughed and screamed together as only an Upward Bound family could.

Chapter 8

THE CHIEF JOSEPH TRAIL

ONE COLD night in January 1988, Isabel and Darlene met in a hotel lobby in Boise for several hours to design a field trip for the following summer that would explore in great detail the compelling Native American history and culture of the region. That year would mark the twentieth anniversary of the Upward Bound program at the University of Idaho, and the women wanted it to be a summer to remember.

They had quite a bit of leeway in designing the curriculum each year, so long as it met the federal guidelines and included math, science, and English as core courses as well as rigorous study hall sessions where students were drilled in effective study habits. But these guidelines did not stipulate where the classes were to take place nor what underlying subject material was used in the lessons. Why not focus the summer classes entirely on Native American subject matter?

Upward Bound had become a rigorous institution on campus. Teachers kept after students until they completed their studies, meeting with them at lunchtime, if necessary, or working closely with them at the end of the day. "I would sometimes even follow them into their dorm rooms at night if I needed to," said Darlene. "We were determined to have them succeed."[1]

By now, getting out and about from classrooms had long been a big part of the program. The summer ahead would take students on eight days of historical immersion along the Nez Perce National Historic Trail, a tour established two years earlier that follows the 1,170-mile trek Chief Joseph took in 1877 in an attempt the allude the US Army.

ROAD TRIP INTO HISTORY

The journey would first take them to Wallowa Lake in the heart of the traditional Nez Perce homeland, the area Chief Joseph and his followers were forced to abandon prior to the 1877 war. From there, they would proceed to ancient sites, battlefields, and other places of historical or cultural significance while studying Nez Perce history and lore, medicines, and myths. Along the way, they would read Merrill D. Beal's *I Will Fight No More Forever*, about the heroic and tragic final battles of the Nez Perce War. "There was so much native history within two hundred miles of Moscow that it just made sense," said Darlene. "We knew the Appaloosa Horse Club took people on rides in many of those areas. Why couldn't we do the same thing with our students?"[2]

The planned journey proved to be a popular idea. Some ninety people, including students, faculty, and a few relatives agreed to go on a five-hundred-mile journey together, from Moscow to Wallowa Lake, and then back to Lewiston and through the Nez Perce Reservation to Kamiah, home of the "upriver" Nez Perce.

There would be several side trips to historic Nez Perce sites in the area. The group would then travel to White Bird Grade, where the first battle took place, and eventually beyond the Lolo Trail to the Big Hole Battlefield. The students would also travel to where, according to legend, the Nez Perce Tribe came into creation and to some places where non-Indians weren't always allowed.

The first few weeks of Upward Bound that summer were spent in the usual fashion on the University of Idaho campus. The girls stayed in Ethel Steel House. The boys stayed one block away in Targhee Hall. Classes started in the morning at eight o'clock sharp; dormitory doors closed at night at ten o'clock sharp, followed by lights out. Students spent their days in a variety of classes: computer programming, math, photography, art, creative writing, journalism, and biology, in addition to the federally required courses. They spent afternoons at sports, playing games around campus, or developing photographic prints in the College of Education darkroom. Some kids went into town. In those days, U of I and WSU had summer stock theaters. A group of students who were interested in seeing the plays could walk to the Hartung Theater on campus after dinner, or pile into the Gray Goose for a drive to Pullman. On Friday nights, staff members often joined students for a loud and exciting roller-skating session in Moscow or Lewiston. The staff loved it as much as the kids.

Stories and photographs from Upward Bound sessions were gathered at the end of each summer into a yearbook. The 1988 yearbook was titled *Taats Timeepnin Tyum*, which means "Happy Summer Memories" in Nez Perce. Many of the memories gathered in that yearbook are included here.

Drama teacher Michael Davis directed some students that summer in a production of the 1950s-era one-act comedy *Listen, Dad*, by playwright Donald Payton. After supper, students attended one hour of mandatory study hall followed by sports of all kinds, including tennis, basketball, and swimming. Junior Tim Stone interviewed John Crout, a physical education teacher and counselor in the boy's dorm who led the Monday night sports program.

> STONE: Why do we need Monday night sports?
> CROUT: You need to work together as a team, and you need to count on each other.
> STONE: What do you think about somebody working by themselves, and not working with the team?
> CROUT: If someone works alone, they will have a rude awakening, because nobody can work by himself.[3]

Darlene had for some time focused her students' attention on Native American stories about Coyote, the Trickster, and other mythical characters and historical places of interest in the region. She and Isabel now planned to expand these studies with site visits.

Darlene used University of Idaho connections to reach out to a group of renowned western writers who were planning a summer workshop in Nez Perce country. Fishtrap: Writing and The West was organized that summer for the first time, gathering the likes of Craig Leslie, William Kittredge, Naomi Nye, Terry Tempest Williams, James Welch, and festival organizer and Oregon poet Kim Stafford. Many of the writers would be staying at the home of famous historian and author Alvin Josephy, near Wallowa Lake, deep in the ancestral homeland of the Nez Perce Tribe.

The Fishtrap conference took its name from the Nez Perce word *wallowa*, which refers to the anchor on each end of traditional fishing weirs, or fish traps. By using this metaphor, it seemed clear that the Fishtrap conference writers held an intention to honor the earliest inhabitants of the region. Darlene took this as an invitation to participate. "I thought the writers who were setting up shop in the Wallowa Valley might want to meet the descendants of Chief Joseph and Looking Glass and others—to meet the original inhabitants of the place," she said.[4]

THE EMISSARY

For the trip to succeed, Isabel and Darlene needed the help of a bona fide emissary from the tribe, someone who was well-versed in its history, language, and legends as well as current events. This person would also need to be familiar with the extended family ties that make up Nez Perce society. They needed Mari Watters. "The first time I met Mari I was a little taken aback," said Darlene. "But I had been told that she knew all there was to know about the Nez Perce. Her trailer was located on the outskirts of Moscow and a bit run down. The window shades were drawn, and smoke and music emanated from within. I probably hesitated before knocking."[5]

Mari came out to meet Darlene with a gregarious hello and the boundless energy she soon brought to Upward Bound as a teacher and guide. People had warned Darlene and Isabel that Mari could sometimes provoke the tribal council with her views and could be didactic toward whites when it came to the importance of Native American culture. "The fact is that not everyone liked her," said Isabel. "But we just loved Mari Watters."[6]

Her hair in pigtails, Mari came out to greet Darlene, wearing a wide grin. She was feminine but also bold and strong, and she was a formidable presence among the students. Mari worked as an Upward Bound teacher for many years, using her position to revitalize the notion of tribal identity in her students while pursuing a master's degree at WSU.

"The US government had been cutting funds for medicine and education for decades," said O.J. Watters, Mari's nephew, who came along on what was now being called "The Chief Joseph Trail Trip of 1988."[7] Today, he works full-time at the Clearwater Casino. "Our treaty is supposed to provide doctors and hospitals for Nez Perce, so my Aunt Mari was trying to keep these promised funds for eyeglasses so kids with poor eyesight could read and go to school," he added.

Mari had earned a degree in cultural anthropology from the U of I and established the first Nez Perce language curriculum at WSU, so Isabel and Darlene decided that having her teach Nez Perce to the students could fulfill the foreign language offering that summer. Once the group hit the road, core lessons in math, science, and English were to be based as much as possible on examples and materials from Nez Perce history and culture.

On the road, students' safety would have to be a primary concern. "I was good at winning the support of families from tribal areas and other towns," said Isabel. "They had to trust me a lot to let me take their kids from them each summer for six weeks. They also had to trust me to make sure that their girls would not get pregnant."[8] Therefore, the boys and girls would camp separated each night and abide by a clearly defined boundary. Because she could persuade students to comply with the rules, Mari was given the title of "whip woman." In Nez Perce society, a whip man would keep order among the seminomadic people by cajoling or "whipping" those youngsters who needed prodding toward completion of their duties. Mari now played this role as a woman.

During the first summer Mari was on staff, Upward Bound had a hickey problem. "Kids were giving each other these big hickeys all over their necks, and it was embarrassing when we went into a store or someplace," said Isabel.[9] Staff decided that stipends would be withheld from any student found with a hickey. This caused such a ruckus that they soon discovered many of the girls were getting hickeys from one single boy, just so the girls would lose their money. Tana Wheeler, one of the students that year who got hickeys, remembered the situation well. "I have to admit, today, that I wasn't exactly a victim," she said.[10]

Mari, in true whip-woman fashion, stepped in to provide a teaching opportunity. According to one story, Mari found the suspect boy, got him on the ground, sat on him, and then started giving him hickeys all over until he understood what it was like. The hickeys ended.

PLANNING AND PACKING

Mari's unconventional teaching methods might have concerned some staff members, but her knowledge of Nez Perce traditions proved indispensable on the Chief Joseph Trail trip. She arranged beforehand a visit to Talmaks Camp, where members of the six original Nez Perce Presbyterian congregations had met each summer since 1897. She also shared Nez Perce myths and legends at many stops along the way, reminding the students that the land held a deep and vital Native American legacy.

Student teacher Greg Torline, a non-native hunter and craftsman, sketched and painted illustrations of the landscapes they traveled through, encouraging students to try their hand at making art. Before leaving campus, some students had joined him in making painted drums of stretched hides, built from scratch during a Native American skills workshop. Torline's favorite saying, quoted in the Upward Bound yearbook for that year, was, "He who does nothing makes no mistakes." Greg Torline, his wife Janet, and their two children were among the many teachers and family members encouraged to go along on the Chief Joseph Trail. Because Greg spent so much time getting Mari from place to place, Mari referred to Janet jokingly as Greg's second wife.

Nez Perce student Tana Wheeler, then fifteen, was the only girl who insisted on joining the boys during drumming sessions on campus. She said that one of her elders, Sam Jackson, had taught her how to sing the old Nez Perce songs when she was thirteen, an age when only a few of the local kids were committed to learning them. "Greg had us soak the hides and stretch them onto a frame with our own hands," said Tana. "At the end of the summer, I showed it to my Grandpa Wally, and he asked if he could hold it for me. I never got it back from him, but that was okay. I knew I would always know where it was."[11]

As news of the plan for the trip got around, the company grew. Students, teachers, scientists, cultural historians, and relatives began to pack for the journey. They would soon board a caravan of automobiles, school buses, and the Gray Goose, bound for a unique learning adventure. The group included science and math teachers Sharon Beidler and her husband Ken Beidler. Darlene's friend and fellow teacher from Hailey, Rudy Boesch, packed a truckload of field equipment, including a five-inch Celestron telescope, microscopes, water test kits, a trunk full of animal skulls to classify, plus equipment that would be used for biological surveys, bird-watching forays, and other environmental studies. Isabel's daughter Paula loaned the group a three-horse trailer that could be filled with food and cooking supplies and kept separate so the kids would not devour all the food before they made camp. Darlene supplied an old pickup trailer that they planned to tow behind the bus and fill with tents, sleeping bags, and packs.

Before departing, the students gathered for two important presentations as part of the study skills class. During presentations, which took place in the large lecture hall on campus, they always took notes. Darlene made notes on an overhead projector so that weaker notetakers could copy them if they missed something. The notes helped them understand the landscape they would soon encounter.

One lecture was delivered by geologist Charles R. Knowles. He had conducted reconnaissance geology and geochemistry surveys of hundreds of thousands of acres in the Idaho back country, from the Bighorn Crags to the Gospel-Hump Wilderness. Knowles supplied an elemental understanding of the slowly changing landscape measured in the epochs of geologic time, providing a new perspective and a broadened time scale of human society and history.

Upward Bound group with elders, 1993. *Private collection. Photograph by Darlene Dyer.*

The other lecture was given by Nez Perce elder and tradition-keeper Horace Axtell (Isluunts). He told the students how he had kept up his Nez Perce language skills while serving in the US Army during World War II by imagining conversations with his grandmother. Axtell's great-grandfather had fought and died in the 1877 Battle of Bear Paw, so he had an emotional attachment to the place where Chief Joseph finally surrendered to the army, ending the fateful flight of his band of cold and starving families as they ran for the Canadian border.

Axtell was known by the honorary title of "Uncle" to many Nez Perce. After marrying his wife Andrea, he had worked for thirty-seven years at the Potlatch Mill in Lewiston while also pursuing the role of cultural tradition-keeper. Many years ago, a group of Nez Perce elders had heard Axtell speaking his language and invited him to learn the old Nez Perce Seven Drum religion. He spent time with other Columbia Plateau tribes while he learned how to conduct the various ceremonies, funerals, and blessings. He also learned how to conduct pipe ceremonies. Axtell was chosen for this work because he already knew the old songs, having learned them from church and from his grandmother.[12]

Axtell's memoir, *A Little Bit of Wisdom*, tells his personal story about growing up Christian while at the same time maintaining a strong tribal identity. Axtell explains in the book how the ceremonial life and spirituality of the Nez Perce, including sweat lodges and longhouse traditions, can go hand in hand with living in mainstream society. "Many religions have been brought to this land," Axtell has been quoted as saying. "And the way my religion is, they teach me, and they taught me, and told me to respect all religions. When someone else believes what his creator is, we can stand and pray together."[13]

Axtell was a great speaker for the students because he witnessed so much of the history they would encounter on their upcoming odyssey. In 1977, one hundred years after the Nez Perce War, Axtell visited the Bear Paw Mountains in Montana, where Chief Joseph formally surrendered. He brought his father along, just two weeks before his death. Axtell's grandfather and three other warriors had escaped toward Canada but decided to return to help Chief Joseph and his followers. All four were shot and killed. The following year, Axtell and Wilfred Scott began conducting memorials at various battle sites along the Nez Perce Trail as well as other locations throughout the ancestral homelands and sites in Kansas and Oklahoma where Nez Perce were held as prisoners after the war.[14]

Along with the lectures and presentations, students read Native American poetry and studied the Heart of the Monster myth, which tells the Nez Perce creation story. The Upward Bound students then journeyed to encounter history firsthand. As much as possible, their classes correlated with Native American ideas and traditions.

Rudy Boesch began teaching the students to identify numerous edible plants along the way, including wild onion, choke cherry, nettles, camas root, and bitterroot. They found examples of blue camas, which was used traditionally as a staple food source, and "death camas," which often grows nearby but is poisonous. "Someone had to have found out the hard way at some time in history that one of them was not an edible plant," said Rudy.[15]

He also provided lessons about medicinal plants used by the Nez Perce prior to European contact, such as willow, which has a pain reliever in its bark, and yarrow, which has also been used for thousands of years in Europe to stop bleeding and aid healing. "Yarrow's genus is *Achillea*, and named after the ancient Greek warrior Achilles," Rudy told his students. "It has been used since the time of Achilles in Europe to help stop bleeding wounds." Rudy told the students that these medicines would surely have been used during the period of bloody conflict between the Nez Perce Tribe and the US Army, the trail of which lay ahead on their journey.[16]

TRACING THE NEZ PERCE TRAIL

Heading south from Moscow across the Palouse, the caravan of cars and buses came to the grand overlook at the confluence of the Snake and Clearwater Rivers, where the huge Scotsman Donald McKenzie built a winter fur trading post in 1812 for John Jacob Astor's Pacific Fur Company. This first outpost was erected only six years after explorers Meriwether Lewis and William Clark arrived in the region and spent six weeks among the Nez Perce at Kamiah. Although the post lasted only a year or two, McKenzie built it to trade specifically with the Nez Perce. It was abandoned in 1813 due to widespread political unrest in the region.[17]

Today, the confluence overlook from the site of McKenzie's post provides a grand view of two great river canyons, the Salmon and Clearwater, as well as the vast Potlatch Mill beside the city of Lewiston, where timber from the region has been used to produce lumber and paper products since 1926. Titans of the timber industry, starting with Charles A. Weyerhaeuser, built a company here that by 1997 included a real estate investment trust with approximately 1.5 million acres of forest land in Arkansas, Idaho, Minnesota, and Wisconsin.[18]

From the overlook, the Chief Joseph Trail caravan headed down miles of switchbacks, across the Clearwater River, and back up through a tangle of valley roads that led through Wallowa-Whitman National Forest toward the towering Wallowa Mountains. To travel through the Wallowa Valley of northeastern Oregon is to be overwhelmed by the stunning beauty of its lakes and rivers, deep gorges, and snow-capped peaks. Lush farm fields and small towns give way to a labyrinth of rolling hills.

A palisade of mountain peaks cupping deep, pristine alpine wilderness reaches into the sky above a verdant plain. Sacagawea Peak, named after the Shoshone woman who helped guide Lewis and Clark on their expedition through the region, and Chief Joseph Mountain mark the skyline within the Eagle Cap Wilderness that feeds the blue-black basin of Wallowa Lake. A visitor to this spectacular region comes quickly to the bittersweet understanding of why Chief Joseph and his band would risk everything to remain here. The Wallowa Valley, with its cool and refreshing mountain breezes that blew across Wallowa Lake, had been the Nez Perce peoples' summer home from time immemorial.

Within a few hours, the group of restless teenagers disembarked on the shores of Wallowa Lake, dispersing to play or help set up camp. Paddleboats and other craft were available for rent. Tame deer walked nearby and allowed themselves to be fed by hand or helped themselves to the camp's supply of peanut butter. Some kids went swimming or played stick games, the ancient indigenous gambling tradition. Others went exploring. Everyone was having fun, glad to be out of the vehicles. As the evening passed, they ate dinner and told stories around the fire until everyone fell asleep, girls on one side and boys on the other.

On Sunday, historian Alvin M. Josephy Jr. came to the Upward Bound breakfast fire with Kim Stafford and novelist James Welch. Welch read from his 1974 novel, *Winter in the Blood*, about an Indian who grew up on the Fort Belknap Reservation in Montana, where the Gros Ventre and Nakota Tribes live. Welch's story about a contemporary man at odds with himself and his white neighbors resonated with the students. The protagonist in the story blames himself for the accidental death of his brother and is haunted by the memory of his father, whom he found dead in a snowdrift. The stark realities of reservation life depicted in the book no doubt struck a chord with some of the Native American students. They were impressed that Welch was both a Native American and a published author, Isabel recalled.[19]

Alvin Josephy, too, had written books about Native Americans, including the Nez Perce. He had attended Harvard, been a war correspondent, and gained renown as a journalist before coming west and dedicating his life to Native American history and culture. He talked to the students about the mountains and the historic events that had taken place there and about some of the tribal stories he had uncovered during his research. Kim Stafford, who directed the Oregon Writing Project at Lewis and Clark College, talked to the students about his mission to record and preserve family memories in his poetry and essays. To set an example, he described for the students an article he had recently written about his grandmother, and he explained the process of keeping a diary and taking careful notes.

The students were then taken on a drive through the town of Joseph, and they toured a foundry where bronze castings for sculptures were made. Students learned the process of casting from guides who also showed them several pieces based on Native American subjects.

Most of the kids were familiar with the area, having spent time there during the Chief Joseph Days Rodeo while they were growing up. Tana Wheeler, now forty-seven, had camped with her family near the rodeo grounds in Joseph when she was a kid. "There would be tipis and tents put up back then," said Tana. "Chief Joseph's headstone is there, so it feels like home to us, not as though we are just visitors. But when we wanted to stay there overnight back then, we got chased away."[20]

That night, some of the students slept in tents while others slept out under the stars on the shores of Wallowa Lake. Some slept in a tipi that the group brought along to set up as they went from place to place. On Monday, the group loaded up once more to drive south, away from the lake. The massive Wallowa Mountains loomed larger and larger behind them as they moved out onto the plain and toward the Talmaks campground, the permanent home and summer gathering place of the six early Presbyterian Nez Perce congregations.

The caravan stopped along the way at Joseph Canyon and the Grande Ronde River, where science teacher Rudy Boesch had students analyze stream samples for biological activity, alkalinity, and other characteristics.

The students and some staff members took the opportunity to jump into the Grande Ronde to cool off. Many of the students had learned to swim at the U of I campus, but jumping into the rushing river posed a new set of challenges. One young boy, a son of one of the instructors, was nearly swept away from the pool and into the current.

The group arrived that evening at Talmaks campground. Situated in a pine forest on Mason Butte, Talmaks is the place where Nez Perce have gathered together in Christian fellowship for over a century. The students were welcomed into the cabins at Talmaks; they ate traditional Indian foods as well as the staple hot dogs and beans that were stashed in the horse trailer. Mari, who had spent time at Talmaks as a young girl, told stories that evening about how the tribe lived in this place many years ago, about the Nez Perce students' grandparents, and some of the silly and embarrassing things their parents had done when they were younger.

Mari told a story in Nimiipuutimt, or Nez Perce, about a young Indian couple, and she translated every line into English for those who did not understand the original:

> The man always went out fishing while the wife stayed home to cook and clean. One night, the young man told his wife, "I am going to go fishing and hunting; I will be back later." She kissed him, and he went on his way. The night got late, and her husband did not come home. His wife had cooked a great meal of salmon, so she decided to eat without him, and after she ate, she fell asleep.
>
> Her husband came home, and he kissed his wife. As he prepared for bed, he asked her, "Wife, what did you cook tonight?" His wife answered, "Fissshhhhh." The husband said, "Oh, my favorite, how many did you eat?" His wife said, "Twwwwooooo." Her husband said in surprise, "Two? You must have been hungry?" His wife said nothing. He reached over and touched her shoulder, and she awoke, happy to see her husband home safe. He looked surprised because he had been talking to her and she had been answering, but he came to find out she had been asleep, and her answers were just gas.

The kids, probably gassy themselves, laughed themselves to sleep that night. On Tuesday morning, the group left Talmaks and headed for Slate Creek, stopping along the way at the Weis Rockshelter, west of Grangeville, where archaeologist and US Forest Service ranger Donna Turnipseed told the story of the region's earliest inhabitants. The students took notes on her lecture, reinforcing their study skills while deepening their understanding of the area's ancient history.

Located near the center of traditional Nez Perce territory, about four miles up Rocky Canyon on the northern edge of the Clearwater Plateau, the Weis Rockshelter was inhabited from eight thousand to two thousand years ago.[21] The cave lies in the midst of camas root-gathering fields and was found to contain a large number of animal bones—mostly deer, bear, bison, sheep, coyote, rodents, and birds. A few fish bones were also found during archaeological digs there, along with artifacts made of worked, rounded river stones; bone and antler tools; shell objects; and piles of obsidian flakes left over from making sharp-edged spear and arrow points. Tana Wheeler picked one up and was amazed at how sharp it was. Because no obsidian can be found in the area around the Weis Rockshelter, it has been surmised that these early inhabitants traveled widely or perhaps traded with distant tribal groups for the dark, glass-like stone.

Following the lecture, the students formed into smaller groups to attend a daily rotation of lessons, from math to English to science. Darlene blew a whistle when it was time for the groups to switch from one instructor to the next.

CHIEF JOSEPH'S DILEMMA

From this prehistoric site, the group traveled up the steep White Bird Grade, above White Bird Canyon, where the first battle of the Nez Perce War took place. It was mid May in 1877 when the non-treaty Nez Perce reluctantly agreed to leave the Wallowa Valley for the trek east to the confines of Lapwai. Unlike the bands of Lawyer and other chiefs, this group had not signed a treaty in 1868 and still lived by the treaty of 1855, which guaranteed access to the Wallowas.[22] Chief Joseph appealed to the commissioners to understand his position in 1876:

> In the treaty councils the commissioners have claimed that our country had been sold to the Government. Suppose a white man should come to me and say, "Joseph, I like your horses, and I want to buy them." I say to him, "No, my horses suit me, I will not sell them." Then he goes to my neighbor, and says to him: "Joseph has some good horses. I want to buy them, but he refuses to sell." My neighbor answers, "Pay me the money, and I will sell you Joseph's horses." The white man returns to me and says, "Joseph, I have bought your horses, and you must let me have them." If we sold our lands to the Government, this is the way they were bought.[23]

The students learned that Joseph's band was given thirty days to clear out of the region. They gathered only basic belongings on travois and thousands of their half-wild horses and cattle, which had long grown accustomed to open range. Allowed to pack only what their animals could carry across the Snake River, they abandoned their household and ranch equipment, boarding rafts made of tight skins to ferry them across the rushing Snake and Salmon Rivers.

Chief Joseph and his band were devastated at the prospect of having to abandon 90 percent of the land that had been promised them under the treaty of 1855 in exchange for allotments in the unfamiliar territory of Lapwai. But white commissioners and Indian agents were determined that Joseph's band be brought to heel, with the idea of "turning these hunters, stockmen, and Dreamers into farmers, husbandmen, and Christians," wrote author Merrill D. Beal.[24] During a final attempt to remain free, Nez Perce medicine man Toohoolhoolzote confronted US representatives at Lapwai, asking provocative philosophical questions about the author of creation, the origin of human species, and the right of one person to coerce another. He was temporarily thrown in the stockade for his insubordination. After Toohoolhoolzote was released, the group of chiefs finally agreed to leave the Wallowa Valley.[25]

On a high vantage point of the old White Bird Grade, the Upward Bound caravan pulled over to hunt for fossils. Mari Watters pointed out to the students the fording place far below where two thousand Nez Perce Appaloosa horses were led across the two-hundred-yard-wide Snake River in 1877 when the river was full of spring runoff. She told them of the first reprisals by young Nez Perce warriors against whites that would soon lead to open warfare, and she performed a traditional Seven Drum prayer, known in the Nez Perce language as Hanyawat. The Seven Drum tradition teaches that the creator made human beings and gave power to Mother Earth, which in turn provides them with plants, animals, and food. For the traditional Nez Perce, everything has a soul, even water. Rituals, drumming and singing, and feasting honor the connection between man and nature.

The Upward Bound students had been reading Beal's account of the 1877 war. Those who did not already know the history of the Nez Perce War from family members were now familiar with the first attacks by young Nez Perce warriors, who by then felt they had little to lose. The Nez Perce had endured twenty-four years of thieving, murder, and oppression by gold miners and cattlemen, many of whom were hardened Civil War veterans. As a result, tribal members had grievances aimed at specific Indian-hating individuals. The forced exodus from the Wallowa Valley to the unfamiliar confines of Lapwai proved too much to bear. Young Nez Perce tribesmen were seething with animosity.[26]

Chiefs Joseph and Ollokut were on the other side of the Salmon River slaughtering beef when young Wahlitits and his cousins Sarpsis Ilppilp and Swan Necklace went raiding on their own, thinking to avenge the murder of Wahlitits's father, Eagle Robe. Numerous whites were killed, most of whom had previously been responsible for the murder or wounding of Nez Perce. Whiskey fueled further attacks, and other warriors from Chief White Bird's band joined in raids. Atrocities were committed, drawing the wrath of the US Army. Beal's book puts into perspective the motivations of these young warriors.[27] "These Nez Perce youths were not degenerates," wrote Beal. "Men of their fire are called patriots when they succeed.

Inevitably, when a combination of pressures brings a liberty-loving people into jeopardy, an explosive situation evolves."[28]

Some of the students were more familiar with the history of these sites than others because they had direct family connections to the terrain and heart-wrenching history that had taken place here. Upward Bound student Josiah Pinkham was along on the trip. His ancestor Eloosykasit, who later in life would be known as John Pinkham, was seventeen years old when the hostilities of 1877 broke out. He and a friend were riding horses to attend the races at Tolo Lake, a Nez Perce gathering place, when the young men were told that a war had begun. They decided to not return home to Chief Timothy's Alpowa band, but instead joined the others in their flight from the US Army and citizen volunteers who were tracking them.[29]

"Thus, they found themselves unwilling members of the noncombatant contingent of the patriot cause," wrote Lucullus Virgil McWhorter in *Yellow Wolf: His Own Words*, an account of the 1877 war as told by Nez Perce witnesses to the battle.[30]

Young Eloosykasit (Standing on a Point) served as an attaché to Wahlitits. A short while later, at White Bird Canyon, below present-day Grangeville, the US Army and citizen volunteers attacked the Nez Perce from above but were routed in a battle defeat that has been compared to Custer's Last Stand at the Battle of the Little Bighorn.[31] Eloosykasit took up a US Army Springfield rifle from a soldier who fell at White Bird and carried it as his weapon, on toward Montana with Chief Joseph and the rest of his followers.

The Battle of White Bird Canyon was the first of several skirmishes that demonstrated to the US Army and the newspaper-reading public that the Nez Perce, despite having elders, women, and youngsters in tow, were not to be trifled with. As they fought on for four months—defeating, eluding, or battling to a draw with the US Cavalry—their plight drew the sympathy of some newspaper readers. The campaign surprised the citizens of the region through whose lands the battles were being fought, ostensibly for their protection. During the conflict,

Joseph's reputation as a statesman grew. "Chief Joseph's magnanimity may save us, and that is all," wrote an editor in the *Lewiston Teller* on June 26, 1877.[32]

SWITCHING TIME SCALES

After Mari's talk and a brief recounting of the events of that day in 1877 when the war began, the students turned their attention to another perspective entirely. They studied ancient fossil beds along the old White Bird Grade, from Grangeville to White Bird, that were deposited millions of years ago when an inland sea covered the area. During the Miocene Epoch, sea creatures, plants, and animals—many of them long extinct—swam, crawled, and grew at the site. Tectonic uplift and eons of erosion pushed these fossilized remains up toward the sky. Each student was instructed to find and identify at least one fossil.

A Nez Perce student found a piece of green chert that had once been used for making arrow and spear points and showed it to science teacher Rudy Boesch, who marveled at the bright green crystals that had grown upon it. "I suggested that he keep it because it was so beautiful," said Rudy. "But he gave it back to me, saying it would mean more to me than it would to him."[33] He has kept the rock to this day; it rests on the mantle in his Hailey, Idaho, home as a reminder of the Chief Joseph Trail trip. "Those kids could be rowdy, you know," said Rudy, who recently retired from teaching. "They also wanted to tease me. At one point they surrounded me when I was standing on a bridge like they were going to throw me over the side, but I knew it was only a joke and a game for them."[34]

Tensions arose during the bus ride down White Bird Grade when Chip White, a charismatic member of the group, pulled a pocketknife on a student teacher on the bus. The bus came to a halt; after some conversation, Darlene tried to assure some members of the staff that Chip's display was not a serious one. When hours later Chip was caught stealing merchandise from a gas station store in Grangeville, the police were called. It became apparent that he could no longer continue on the

Upward Bound student Jack Zachary setting up camp, 1993.
Private collection. Photograph by Darlene Dyer.

journey, so Darlene and Gail stayed behind with him at a police station until his mother arrived several hours later to take him home.

Darlene and Gail caught up with the group at Slate Creek Ranger Station on US Highway 95, where the group had received permission months before to set up a tipi and camp. The site is not far from where Chief Joseph reflected in June 1877 on what might lay ahead for his band. Although he was powerless in the egalitarian society of the Nez Perce people to control the actions of young warriors, he was also trusted to help lead his people to safety.

At Slate Creek, the students used a meeting hall to make popcorn and watch a film version of *I Will Fight No More Forever*. The young men then split into teams to play a game of football. Late that night, Mari told ghost stories around the campfire before the boys and girls went to their respective sides of the camp to sleep.

In the morning, a group of students, led by their science teacher, climbed a steep trail about 150 feet above the valley floor to a limestone cave beside a spring that had been used as a shelter by indigenous people prior to European contact. Called the Lucile Caves, Rudy told them that this area was known by scientists to contain a rare type of ground snail, the *Oreohelix*, as long ago as 1860—some seventeen years before Chief Joseph battled the US Army in the area. In this way, Upward Bound students encountered both traditional Native American and Western scientific worldviews, which grew to complement one another as the trip progressed.

After returning, the group packed into buses and cars for the drive to the Clearwater High School athletic field in Kooskia for daily classes in English, math, and science, and then made a short stop at the 1920s-era Lochsa Historical Ranger Station. Near Lochsa in 1806, Lewis and Clark's Corps of Discovery took a break from their struggle westward across the Lolo Pass. According to a historical marker, one member of the expedition described the Lolo Trail area as "this horrible mountainous desert." The trail had been used by the Nez Perce for trading and buffalo hunting with neighboring tribes to the east. "Hungry, dejected and desperate, the men of the Corps crossed this endless sea of mountains," continued the marker. "Today, you see no trail through this area. Downed trees and bog make travel treacherous on foot or by horse."[35]

Yet, 150 years ago, the Lolo Trail was a secret way across the mountains to Montana. While camped near here with the Corps of Discovery along Hungry Creek, Lewis and Clark's Nez Perce guides performed a fire ceremony, torching tall fir trees to ensure good weather for their journey. "They are a beautiful object in this situation at night," wrote Meriwether Lewis, who was reminded of a display of fireworks.[36] The Nez Perce then skillfully led the expedition to safety. "We were entirely surrounded by those mountains from which to one unacquainted with them it would have seemed impossible ever to have escaped . . . these fellows are most admireable pilots," wrote Lewis.[37]

GHOST TIPIS

Fifty years later, by late summer of 1877, Chief Joseph and his families and warriors were running for this western end of the Lolo Trail in the hope that they could hide in its desolate reaches from the US military. They planned to head east into buffalo country, where Chief Looking

Glass expected to find support from the Crow Tribe. Instead, they found that the Crows had already seen the writing on the wall and aligned themselves with the US military to safeguard their own survival.[38]

The Upward Bound group took roads that roughly followed the Lolo Trail route, then proceeded eastward on Highway 12 to Lee Creek Campground in Montana. After dinner, some of the older kids took younger, more impressionable campers for a snipe hunt before settling down to a good night's rest. On Thursday, they awoke to a cold and rainy day and ate a pancake and orange juice breakfast before stuffing themselves once more into the caravan of buses and automobiles for the long drive south to the Big Hole Battlefield, about ten miles from Wisdom, Montana.

The caravan arrived at a campground within sight of a gathering of "ghost tipis" erected in memorial to the many families who camped there on August 9, 1877, after the arduous trek along the Lolo Trail from Idaho to Montana. The students then set up camp and toured the Big Hole National Battlefield visitor center, where historians have endeavored to make sense of a battle that led to the tragic deaths of many people.

The Battle of the Big Hole brought sorrow to both sides in one of the last few Indian wars of the western frontier. Numbering about 750 persons in all, with about 200 warriors, the Nez Perce had successfully eluded General Oliver O. Howard's forces and peacefully traded with nearby residents before camping in an undefended area of the Big Hole to replenish their supply of tipi poles. Unknown to the Nez Perce, Colonel John Gibbon had left Fort Shaw, near Great Falls, Montana, with 161 officers and men and one twelve-pound howitzer capable of firing at a range of almost one mile. Gibbon had orders to take no prisoners and not engage in negotiations.[39]

At dawn on August 9, Gibbon and his men walked toward eighty-nine tipis pitched in willows on the North Fork of the Big Hole River, killing an old Nez Perce man they encountered along the way. The soldiers met what remained of Chief Joseph's people, including the families of Yellow Wolf and White Bird, as well as Looking Glass, who had been drawn into the conflict after soldiers raided his village. Gibbon attacked while many of the families were still sleeping and tried to burn the tipis, but he soon found himself in an untenable position as warriors, many of whom died protecting their families, regrouped at the northern end of the camp and made a counterattack. The howitzer fired twice before it was captured by Nez Perce warriors and dismantled.[40] Meanwhile, the women, children, and elders packed up to flee the camp while warriors moved into position around the army's rifle pits on a wooded hillside.

Colonel Gibbon recalled many years later the moment when scattered Nez Perce managed to return to their tipis: "Few of us will soon forget the wail of mingled grief, rage, and horror which came from the camp four or five hundred yards from us when the Indians returned to it and recognized their slaughtered warriors, women, and children."[41]

The Upward Bound students took their classes that day near the Big Hole Battlefield on tables beside the museum. Every forty minutes, Darlene blew a whistle and the students rotated from science class to math, and then English lessons. Students also toured the museum, which provided a detailed history of the site and displays of important Nez Perce artifacts. The battlefield casualties had been memorialized in exquisite detail by historians eager to represent the facts for future generations. Red wooden markers in the shape of feathers showed the locations of fallen Nez Perce warriors while blue markers in the shape of military caps marked the locations of fallen US soldiers.

For English class that day, Darlene supplied Kim Stafford's essay, "A Few Miles Short of Wisdom," about his own visit to the Big Hole Battlefield only a few years before: "What did I expect? The past wears an armor that thickens, and I was a fool to think hunger and a wish could pierce it. I had learned the dates and the map, had seen in photographs a long-braided woman and the anguish of old men. I had browsed on books at the National Battlefield gift shop, and I was fed full with history and the news that stays facts."[42]

Stafford wrote that a ranger had taken him into confidence, telling him of secret ceremonies that took place on the Big Hole Battlefield at night, how people surreptitiously came to pay respects by tying ribbons on trees at the place where Five Wounds died.

Also known as Pahkatos Owyeen, Five Wounds had been wounded in the right hand at the Battle of the Clearwater. For many years, he fought beside Rainbow, or Wahchumyus, a war leader of the non-treaty Nez Perce. The fathers of both men had died on the same day in battle many years before. Therefore, they made a pact that should one die in battle, the other would also die.[43] Stafford wrote:

> When I found the ribbons, they were red and blue. Five strands flickered half a fathom long from a single branch of the pine growing where Five Wounds died. The ribbons knotted at eye level swung new in the breeze, and between my feet a single strand of older ribbon had fallen, bleached white by snow and sun. The age of this custom made me dizzy. The five ribbons on the limb were new as the soft needle-growth sprung from the pine candles. The faded ribbon on the ground lay among the sun-bleached needles. The sun-white ribbon on the ground took me back to the hopeful recollections of bead, fur, and photograph cased in glass at the museum, while the five new ribbons conveyed me to the ceremonies of the night.[44]

Five Wounds chose to die that day after learning that Rainbow had fallen, shot in the neck. He took his time to mourn his fallen friend before taking up a rifle, having a swig of whiskey from a fallen soldier's canteen, and walking up the hill toward the army's rifle pits, and to his certain death.[45]

Stafford wrote that he had remained transfixed by the sight, "so long the sun moved and a cool shadow rose out of the ground . . . a century collapsed into this moment of ground, where generations of private celebration grew outward from one story. This square yard of pine duff bound a guest register that could never be tallied, only renewed, only inhabited by the night-faithful memory that walked in the form of the people."[46]

Stafford realized the difference between knowing history from a display or brochure and feeling a part of it deep in one's soul. "All of that can make a visitor ready to know. But a public way is not knowing in itself, only a preparation for knowing. Knowing is a change of heart, physical, slower than the eye's travel across a page of text, or across a stone dressed with words," he wrote.[47]

The ribbons that Stafford had seen at the Big Hole Battlefield several years earlier were no longer in evidence when the Upward Bound group arrived. So, before each English lesson ended, Darlene cut sections of colored ribbon for each student. They were permitted to walk back to the battlefield to tie the ribbons at places that were sacred or important to them, transforming history and study into a personal ritual.

Of all the tragic events that transpired during the Battle of the Big Hole, perhaps the most heartbreaking is the story of Josiah Pinkham's ancestor, Wahlitits, and his wife. An account of the tragedy was told by Pinkham's ancestor, Eloosykasit (Standing on a Point, later known as John Pinkham), to Lucullus McWhorter. Because Eloosykasit was a relative, he had camped beside that warrior's family at the Big Hole in 1877 the night before Colonel Gibbon and his men attacked. Assured by Chief Looking Glass that they were out of harm's way, the families were at ease on the night before the battle. For two months, Wahlitits had carried the US Army rifle he had taken from a fallen soldier after the Battle of White Bird Canyon, using it to defend his family and wife, who was with child.

"At the Big Hole camp, the Indians had a great time the night before the attack," Eloosykasit told McWhorter. "They paraded and sang all through the camp. Some were gambling at a stick, or bone, game near some brush. When the attack came, just before daylight, Wahlitits and his wife ran to a shallow depression fronting their tepee," only twenty steps from where soldiers were charging toward them out of the willows.[48] Wahlitits implored her to run to join the others. When she stood up, she was shot and fell back down by his side. "He called out before the people, before the warriors, 'My wife is shot to die! I will not leave her! I will go nowhere! I am staying here until I am killed!'"[49]

Eloosykasit said a soldier then broke through the willows and was dropped by Wahlitits with a single bullet. Wahlitits was then killed by another soldier who shot him in the face. "I did not see what I now tell, but others told me this about his wife," said Eloosykasit. "Though bad wounded, she reached her husband's rifle and killed the soldier who had shot him. She was then quickly killed by other soldiers. A good-looking woman, she was soon to be a mother."[50]

Only four steps away from Wahlitits and his wife, Wahchmuyus (Rainbow) lay flat on the ground, shooting at the soldiers in the willows. He was killed by a rifle shot in the neck. After discovering that Rainbow lay dead, Pahkatos Owyeen (Five Wounds) cried in despair over his fallen friend. "Pahkatos, a great warrior, was well-known among the Sioux. A man of strong feeling, strong in battle. Never was known to cry and show tears," recalled Chief Ollokot's wife, Wetatonmi, speaking to McWhorter of the two great warriors' last day in battle. She shared her memories with McWhorter before she died in 1934.[51]

"Rainbow lay dead where the fighting had been hard. He and Pahkatos had grown up together. Always went together when hunting buffalos or on war path. Had never been separated for long. He cried over his friend. Cried long. He said, 'This sun, this time, I am going to die. My brother is killed and I shall go with him.'" Pahkatos then showed his bravery to the rest of his tribe's defenders when he took his rifle toward the soldier's trenches. "The first shots missed him. The next shots he fell dead," said Wetatonmi.[52]

The loss of these two great warriors was a deep blow, yet their brave resistance allowed the remaining Nez Perce to repel the soldiers long enough to assess a scene of devastating carnage; children burned alive in tepees, old people shot and killed, a mother lying dead with a mortally injured infant still screaming at her breast. Sergeant Charles N. Loynes of the Seventh Infantry participated in the battle. Many years later, he wrote a letter to McWhorter describing what he witnessed, saying it was the most pitiful scene of his military career:

> The Indian woman of whom I told you I saw lying dead with a baby on her breast as it swung its little arm back and forth—the lifeless hand flapping at the wrist broken by a bullet—was outside the tepee. When

> I think of those terrible scenes, wrongs waged against human beings, I say shame! Shame! This great Christian government had power to do differently by those truly patriotic people. It is such remembrances which touch my emotions, and I am led to marvel at the term "civilization."[53]

At Mari Watters' insistence, several students in the group were allowed by Nez Perce National Historic Park officials to camp for one night out on the Big Hole Battlefield. They included Josiah Pinkham, Trulin Ellenwood, Cindy Lou Wilson, Bea and Tana Wheeler, Becca Miller, Deanne Bear, Russ Nida, Mike Taylor, and Lawrence "Mo" Abrahamson. Counselor Ronald A. Moses stayed with them on the battlefield. They camped in the trees above the "ghost tipis" on the battlefield made of bare tipi poles. "Mari insisted that the park rangers allow us to stay out there," said Josiah Pinkham. "She also told us that we would be expected to behave correctly, that some of our ancestors had fought and died there."[54]

Long after the smoke from the Battle of the Big Hole had cleared and the war was over, Josiah Pinkham's ancestor, Eloosykasit, inherited the rifle that Wahlitits had used to defend his family before he was shot and killed—the rifle Wahlitits's pregnant wife used to avenge her husband's death before she and her unborn child also died.

Isabel remembered many years later that the place had a solemnizing effect on the students. "They were pretty quiet at the Big Hole Battlefield," she said. "They knew it was a place of the dead and therefore a sacred place."[55]

Janet Torline was summoned in the morning by Mari for a ride out to see how the kids had fared during the night. "The culmination of the entire trip was at the Big Hole Battlefield," Janet said. "But when we showed up, there were giant US flags blowing in the breeze on a typically windy Montana day. Because of what had happened here in 1877, they didn't seem appropriate. It was horrendous."[56]

Janet drove Mari out to the battlefield to hold a ceremony. They drove through a rising mist that could have been mistaken for gun smoke and heard sandhill cranes clacking nearby, recalled Janet:

We heard a coyote bark and Mari said, "That's our welcome." Then she circled the kids up and with her eagle feather fan called upon the Great Spirit to be present and bring blessings on these young people. She expressed gratitude for the opportunity to be here. The kids who were usually very active and happy were all quite somber after spending the night out there.

Mari asked the group what they had to say, and one of the Nez Perce boys said he hadn't realized until that night that his family had a connection to that place and that he felt the connection for the first time. A white boy said he was ashamed of his ancestors after learning of what took place, and he apologized. He thanked Mari and the others for not holding it against him for being who he is.

In 1877, after the Battle of the Big Hole, General Howard's larger force came to the aid of Gibbon, who was injured in the fight, and the pursuit of the Nez Perce continued. The Indians continued on to the Yellowstone area, known to the Nez Perce people as Old Woman's Country, and to the territory of the Crow Tribe, where Looking Glass and Toohoolhoolzote thought they would find an ally against the army. This turned out not to be the case.[57]

By now, the group knew that no place in the country would be safe for them, that they must try to make it across the Canadian border. Chief Sitting Bull had found refuge there after the battle against Custer at the Little Bighorn a year earlier. But winter was now fast approaching, and the Nez Perce had many wounded. Their flight through Yellowstone National Park, established only a few years earlier at the dawn of a new era, went badly. A number of men within a family group of tourists they encountered in the park were captured and killed for trying to escape. More skirmishes followed. The Nez Perce now ran desperately, fighting sporadically, until they gathered at the Bear Paw Mountains, where Looking Glass was shot in the head and killed. Chief Joseph, fearing for the remaining members of his cold and starving band, gave his most enduring speech after this battle:

> Tell General Howard I know his heart. What he told me before, I have it in my heart. I am tired of fighting. Our Chiefs are killed; Looking Glass is dead, Ta Hool Hool Shute is dead. The old men are all dead. It is the young men who say yes or no. He who led on the young men is dead. It is cold, and we have no blankets; the little children are freezing to death. My people, some of them, have run away to the hills, and have no blankets, no food. No one knows where they are—perhaps freezing to death. I want to have time to look for my children, and see how many of them I can find. Maybe I shall find them among the dead. Hear me, my Chiefs! I am tired; my heart is sick and sad. From where the Sun now stands, I will fight no more forever.[58]

Josiah Pinkham has long since graduated from Upward Bound and now serves as an ethnographer for the Nez Perce Tribe. He traveled to Alaska a few years ago to check in on his uncle, ninety-four-year-old Alex Pinkham Jr., who was blind and lived alone outside Anchorage near the cabin he dwelled in when he first homesteaded there in the 1950s after serving in World War II. "He is the patriarch of our family," said Josiah. "His wife has passed, and he can no longer see, but that is where and how he wants to live. I can only hope that I am still able to take care of myself like that when I am his age."[59]

Pinkham's uncle had in his possession the US Cavalry rifle taken from a fallen US soldier at the Battle of White Bird Canyon by Wahlitits, who was killed at the Big Hole, along with his wife, on a battlefield that resonates through time with the tragedies of a displaced people, their sacrifices, and the horrors of war. Alex Pinkham died in January 2020, and now Josiah is responsible for keeping this rifle. It has been passed down in his family for generations. Eloosykasit, known later as John Pinkham, told Lucillus McWhorter in 1940 just how important the rifle had become to his family: "Sometimes when I think of my relations gone, I take up this gun and look at it. Then they come to me and I feel better. I can never give up this gun."[60]

REGROUP AND REFLECT

The Upward Bound group dispersed after camping at the Big Hole on a Friday, the last day of the trip. They were grateful to be headed for warm showers and good food. As a treat, Isabel brought them all to McDonalds, where they each received a four-dollar coupon to spend. The students then split up for the weekend, the northbound group toward Coeur d'Alene and the southbound group to Three Devils Campground for a refreshing swim. The students regrouped the following Monday in Moscow to reflect on the trip and continue their lessons.

Grant Adair, a Nez Perce student from Lapwai, wrote Isabel a letter on June 18, thanking her for an experience that opened his eyes to the complicated history of the region. "This trip did a lot for me personally and education-wise," Adair wrote. "On this trip, I finally learned what it is like to be free of discrimination and feel free in my life. The trip to the Big Hole Battlefield opened a new perspective on the troubling history of Indian/European relations, and upon war in general. From my perspective, seeing all of the casualties of both whites and Indians, it made me wonder why it all happened. I may never know, but at least I got the chance to see the sites of battle during the war, and because of this I would like to thank you."[61]

Even students with no Nez Perce ties discovered during the 1988 Upward Bound session a feeling of compassion for those people who live under the legacy of colonialism and institutionalized racism. Back at the University of Idaho campus, they learned from news reports about the oppressive and racist apartheid regime in South Africa. A movement was underway to pressure universities and colleges across the United States to divest funds from companies doing business in South Africa. The divestment movement was intended to pressure the white minority South African government into abolishing apartheid, which segregated the country and did not extend equality or civil rights to black South Africans.[62]

Anti-apartheid activists there had captured the sympathy of many people around the world who were advocating for sanctions against a regime that kept 90 percent of its population disenfranchised politically. Black South Africans were living removed from modern conveniences on bantustans, or reservations for people of color, while most of the white minority lived with all modern conveniences in relative luxury.

Upward Bound student Albert Penney resolved to write a letter to South Africa's President P. W. Botha, asking for amnesty for the so-called Sharpeville Six, a group of six black South Africans sentenced to death for the 1984 killing of Kuzwayo Jacob Dlamini, the deputy mayor of the city of Sharpeville. In 1960, Sharpeville was the site of a police massacre of protesters seeking an end to the apartheid regime. Police opened fire on about 5,000 unarmed protesters, killing 69 people, including 8 women and 10 children, and injuring 180 others, many of whom were shot in the back as they turned to flee.[63] The story of the Sharpeville Massacre resonated with Albert Penney, who had just visited the Big Hole Battlefield.

Upward Bound teachers taught about what was happening in South Africa, how sentencing the Sharpeville Six to death was considered by many people around the world as an act of vengeance toward black protesters. Penney joined his voice with thousands of others in calling for their freedom, a collective voice that eventually led to the end of the apartheid regime in South Africa. In his 1988 letter to the South African president, Penney wrote: "Your Excellency, I think that it is really unfair that you are punishing them for something that you really can't prove that they did. Human Rights are something that should be known throughout the world. The Sharpeville Six are really being denied these rights and should be set free until proven guilty. I really hope this letter finds them in their time of fear, Sincerely, Albert Penney."[64]

HAPPY SUMMER MEMORIES

Only when the summer was over did some students realize what a positive experience they had shared together. "Upward Bound is our summer home, and Isabel is our summer mother," wrote Victoria Lynn One Bear on the 1988 Upward Bound yearbook's title page. "From the first day, when we were scared, shy, bashful, to our last day, crying to part with friends, our days are full of joy and happiness and togetherness as a family." But not every memory contained in the yearbook is as idyllic as One Bear's. "Algebra class is just about as interesting as ants on an ant hill," wrote one student, anonymously.[65]

Some kids dropped out altogether—or were asked to leave—including Chip White, the charismatic Nez Perce–African American boy from Juliaetta to whom the class and staff ultimately dedicated the 1988 yearbook. Tragedy struck the group and the Nez Perce Tribe later that summer when it was discovered that Chip White, after returning home, had drowned in the Clearwater River. "We taught Chip how to swim that summer as almost all the kids went to the university pool after classes were over for the day, but perhaps only well enough to get himself into trouble," said Darlene many years later. "Maybe he had the confidence to jump in the river but did not have the skill to survive."[66]

Darlene was moved by the tragic death of Chip White to write a poem in the style of Gwendolyn Brooks, a poet she admired, who wrote in simple and powerful verse about the world around her, poems Darlene often shared with Upward Bound students. Brooks had once been quoted as saying: "Art hurts. Art urges voyages—and it is easier to stay at home."

YOU BE TOUGH

You be tough with the teacher
And she call your mom
You be tough with the store clerk
And she call you thief
You be tough talk with the lady cop
And she call you to court
You be tough with the river
And she call you hers.

—D. Matson (for Chip), July 26, 1988

"We don't know everything that happened the day Chip died," said Darlene. "I just remember thinking that there was so much more he could have learned. As teachers, we put so much energy into his education. I thought he still had more summers to spend with Upward Bound. When students do not come back to us, it is easy to think we did not help them enough."[67]

Greg Torline, now sixty-nine, lives off the grid on the edge of Lake Coeur d'Alene, where he and his wife Janet first camped in a tent before building a home. His life as an artist and teacher led to a career as a carpenter. He said the Chief Joseph Trail trip and Native American culture in general have had an impact on his life. Torline hunts with a bow that he made himself, and he enjoys flint-knapping and beadwork.

"I was most impressed that summer with the struggle that Mari Watters was in to get the Indian kids connected to who they were, their history and culture. Mari took us under her wing also," he reflected. "Now that I look back on those days, I realize that I have chosen a path with heart. We realize, too, that all things have a being, and we understand our relationship to Mother Earth. It's not about skin color. When you participate in activities that bring people together, you realize that we are all the same. My ancestors in Germany were living like Native Americans twenty thousand years ago. This is not something new."[68]

PART II

RETHINKING HISTORY

Chapter 9

FAITH

OLLICUTT "O.J." Watters stepped out of his Toyota Tacoma at a convenience store in Lapwai wearing a wide-brim black cowboy hat and black cowboy boots. An eagle foot dangled from the truck's rearview mirror. Between its talons hung a small black marble, a souvenir from an Upward Bound field trip to the Hanford Nuclear Site many years ago. Scientists at Hanford explained the facility's ongoing mission and gave each student a small black marble.

"They said they were still working with uranium to find a way to reduce the half-life of the nuclear waste and at the same time increase the amount of power they could get from nuclear fuel pellets," said O.J. "We learned how the nuclear waste was dumped on the ground in these barrels and how they have been trying to clean it up ever since. We were given these dark marbles and told that they had been crystal clear before they were shot through with radiation."[1]

Now mostly decommissioned, Hanford was created in 1943 to help build the first atomic bombs, which the United States dropped over Japan. During the Cold War, Hanford was expanded to include several nuclear reactors and plutonium processing plants. In 1986, it was made public that nuclear waste from Hanford had been released secretly onto the ground and into the Columbia River for decades, sparking protests from surrounding communities, including the Nez Perce Tribe.[2]

A short drive from the convenience store onto an unmarked side road off the highway is a sturdy wooden structure near some trees—a community sweat lodge on Lapwai Creek. Underneath the structure squatted a domed, willow-stick sweat lodge covered in blankets of all colors and surrounded by benches, couches, and stacks of wood. "We have sweats here for men and for women. Some are spiritual, and some are just for getting together and sweating," O.J. noted. "There are many different religions here on the reservation today. We have Catholics, Baptists, Methodists . . . and we have traditional religions."[3]

After high school, O.J. went to the University of Idaho for a few semesters in 1988 and 1989 on Pell Grants, which he said paid almost all his expenses. "I went to every class and read book chapters, but then I hit the night life. I got incompletes." When he was a boy, O.J. stood in resistance with relatives and others from the community against state officials at Rapid River over Nez Perce treaty fishing rights. He later spent time on wildland firefighting crews and worked for the Nez Perce Department of Fisheries.

In 2001, he returned to U of I for two more semesters, working to complete a sociology degree. "My grades were a lot better when I went there with my own money," he said. "I drove fifty miles from my house, but it became difficult economically to drive back and forth and also have enough food to eat, so I haven't gone back. The course work was good, but economically it was rough for me."[4] O.J. recalled a friend at U of I who packed a Bible around with him to classes, just in case he was confronted by evangelicals who tried to convert him to their religion: "When they quoted Scripture to us, my friend would answer with a quote from a different verse that completely contradicted what the evangelical was saying."

After the Spalding Drum group that O.J. traveled with as a teenager had faded away, he continued to travel with his father's cousin to enjoy Nez Perce homeland areas away from Lapwai. He grew up hearing stories about his ancestors' interactions with missionaries. "When I was growing up, the Spalding Cemetery had a park office [in the former Blue Lantern

Motel nearby] that showed old films. But we heard some stuff from elders that was not in the history at the visitor center," he said.[5]

O.J. said his father found some letters that Henry Spalding and Marcus Whitman, also a missionary, wrote to one another about converting the Nez Perce people to Christianity while teaching them to farm. "Henry Spalding would only give potatoes with seeds on them—the ones that would sprout—to the Christian Indians, but gave bad potatoes away to the non-Christians," O.J. paraphrased. "With no little roots, the potatoes would not grow, and Spalding would say it was because God was angry that they were not Christian."[6]

Examples of tactics such as these were described recently during interviews with Nez Perce elders conducted by Josiah Pinkham and Nakia Williamson. Spalding apparently did not understand that the Nez Perce had a religion of their own. He considered all traditional spiritual beliefs to be "sorcery," and he aimed to put an end to gambling, dancing, and horseracing while introducing the novel concept of "hell" to the tribe.[7]

The landscape of spiritual traditions in Indian Country is diverse, and Wilma Lawrence, a fifty-six-year-old woman from Lapwai, is an example of someone who has availed herself of several. One of fourteen children in her family, six of whom survive today, Wilma worked when she was fourteen at the Lapwai summer youth program before joining Upward Bound in 1977. She remained in the program until she graduated high school in 1981. "We had a lot of fun at Upward Bound, meeting a lot of different friends from different reservations. Some of us still keep in touch."[8]

Wilma has three children and six grandchildren. She worked at the Wild Horse Casino in Pendleton, Oregon, and at an army base. "The accounting classes I took at Upward Bound really helped me. On the weekend, if we did not want to go home, we went on camping trips to Selway Falls," she said. "But it was kind of embarrassing when you got picked up by Isabel in this big car we called the Gray Goose."[9]

Wilma and her family attended powwows and kept up on tribal fishing rights issues. She spent time with the Nez Perce Seven Drum singing group.

Although baptized Catholic, she has attended her mother's Presbyterian church in Kamiah. Her brother, James Homer Allen, was a Sun Dancer. When James died tragically by suicide some years ago, Sun Dance medicine men came to conduct a ceremony at his funeral in Juliaetta, Idaho. That is when Wilma found solace in a tradition that stands outside of both Nez Perce and mainstream Christian religious traditions, one that allows for interaction with the spirit world. During the ceremony, the windows in the house were covered to keep out the sunlight. The indoor lights were turned off before the ceremony began.

"It was a completely new experience for us," Wilma explained. "We had to be totally in the dark. These men explained to us everything that was happening, and we could feel things going by in the room. They told us everything that had happened to Jimmy." The medicine men burned sage and performed other rituals to learn and communicate what they knew to Wilma and her immediate family members. "They made us understand what happened, that although my brother killed himself, by the time he did this he was no longer able to think about us and the effect it would have on us. It helped us to understand that his suicide was not our fault."[10]

The Sun Dance, once banned by federal authorities in the United States, came originally from western Plains tribes. Other traditions practiced on the Nez Perce Reservation are from closer to home. Former Upward Bound student and Nez Perce Tribe ethnographer Josiah Pinkham said the beliefs and practices of the so-called Dreamers of the 1870s, which once drew ire and suspicion from whites, have remained an integral part of Nez Perce culture to this day. "Nez Perce religion is a very big topic," said Josiah. "But it is easy enough to point out that medicine dances and the Seven Drum religion are still a part of our culture."[11]

CHALLENGING THE HISTORICAL RECORD

Josiah undertakes for the tribe a dynamic set of responsibilities, fulfilling federally funded mandates as well as unpaid tasks that involve the perpetuation of Nez Perce culture. He responds to outside requests for information about the tribe while compiling and protecting oral histories. Some of these tribal histories are changing the accepted historical record. He also works to identify and reclaim Nez Perce artifacts from museums around the country.

A notable example of this repatriation process is the return of ceremonial clothes and artifacts now on display at the Nez Perce National Historic Park near Spalding. The tribe bought the materials for $675,000 from the Ohio State Historical Society in 1996 to ensure their continued preservation.[12] They could be worth millions of dollars to a collector, but they have a priceless significance to the tribe. "The real context for Nez Perce material culture is ceremony," said Josiah. "For me, this has become a life's work."[13]

Josiah's understanding of Nez Perce culture and history led him to question some of the presumptions made by writers and historians. His perspective dates from well before the earliest contact between the tribe and explorers Meriwether Lewis and William Clark during their excursion into Nez Perce territory in 1805. He explained that, long ago, the Nimiipuu used to take young people out and away from the villages to fast and seek some kind of power for themselves. These young people would ask for spiritual guidance, and some of them would develop the ability to prophecy. After these spiritual ordeals, the young people would return to paint symbols about their experience on rock walls. These petroglyph designs, which can be found across North America, have bewildered and inspired generations of anthropologists. "These symbols were very personal and esoteric," noted Josiah. "A person could take an entire lifetime trying to interpret his symbol."[14]

Josiah said one Nez Perce prophet saw that the tribe would one day be changed forever by the arrival of a creature that resembled a deer and allowed for easy travel. "This turned out to be the horse," he said.[15] Horse culture for western tribes began to flourish after a 1680 Pueblo Indian revolt in Santa Fe against the Spanish led to the release of numerous horses that were then captured, bred, and traded by western tribes.[16] The Nez Perce became particularly adept at horse breeding, producing the multicolored Appaloosa, which is known for intelligence, speed, and fortitude in battle.

Josiah said a second prophecy foresaw the arrival of white people who looked like the Nimiipuu but had upside-down faces and eyes "like a fish," the color of fading blue and green seen in fish eyes that have been removed from the water. These creatures would bring even bigger change and great suffering to the people. "These were white people," noted Josiah. "They had blue eyes. Many of them were trappers who wore long beards and had bald heads. This is why they were said to have upside-down faces." Josiah added that, for many generations, the tribe discussed the changes, both good and bad, that these prophecies would bring. "The Nez Perce are a peace-loving people, but we have also always been quite the warriors when it comes to defending what is important and what is right."[17]

Josiah has studied the written record of contact between his tribe and Europeans, and he takes issue with a long-held account by historians who claim that Presbyterian ministers were summoned to Nez Perce country by tribal emissaries during the 1830s. Nez Perce oral history states otherwise. "It is true," he said, "that four Nez Perce traveled to St. Louis in search of something, but they weren't looking for the Bible, any type of Christianity, or even religion."[18]

When Lewis and Clark first arrived in Nez Perce country, starving and vulnerable after crossing the mountainous Lolo Trail, the tribe took them in. Josiah said that William Clark's sexual appetite was relatively subdued while in the Corps of Discovery, but he nevertheless fathered a child with Red Bear's sister during his stay with the Nez Perce. "The Nez Perce have always been savvy about maintaining relationships with those outside the tribe, and so it was with William Clark. It was always thought that he would return to be with his child. When he never came back, people eventually said, 'Okay, let's go and find him.'"[19]

Josiah added that the emissaries had another reason to seek out Clark. They sought a kind of magic that they knew would be most valuable, something Clark had shown them thirty years before. "He could write line after line of these small characters and symbols on a page. Then he would give it to someone who wasn't there, and that person could read back what was written. Can you imagine the impact this had on people's minds then? People worked so hard for one symbol and gave a lifetime of commitment to its meaning, and here were people who could string together many of them and fill pages. On top of that, others could speak it back when they weren't there when it was created. It was powerful."[20] Josiah said Clark had promised the tribe in 1805 that he would share the magic of reading and writing with them, but he failed to return to bring this gift to the tribe.

"When the emissaries found Clark in St. Louis, where he was serving as superintendent of Indian Affairs, there was a big problem of communication," noted Josiah. "Clark had long ago forgotten what little Nez Perce he had learned. The emissaries tried to use sign language to describe what they wanted." Somehow, the record of that encounter came to describe the Nez Perce emissaries as people who longed for Christianity and risked their lives to travel east in search of the Bible. "This is completely erroneous," Josiah emphasized. "They were seeking the ability to read and write."[21] Nevertheless, the Presbyterian Church led a mission to what became Spalding, Idaho, where Reverend Henry Spalding and his wife Eliza changed the tribe forever, eventually splitting those who espoused the divinity of Christ from those traditional groups who would henceforth be considered pagan and therefore beyond the pale.

Education can provide choices as well as new perspectives on history and the future. Josiah Pinkham's extended family includes people who are Christian and others who follow the traditional Nez Perce religion. His family includes keepers of tradition as well as scientists with postgraduate degrees working to protect natural resources.

Chapter 10

UPRIVER

ABOUT A one-hour drive northeast from Lapwai is the town of Kamiah on the Clearwater River, home to what are called the "upriver" Nez Perce. On the southeast side of town, across the highway from the Kamiah/Clearwater River KOA Campground and Lewis and Clark Motel, a wooden fence circles the Heart of the Monster. On a misty Sunday morning, the pasture that surrounds this Nez Perce National Historical Park site is empty, except for a pair of geese floating on a pond beside the river. The forty-foot-tall mound of basalt stones that is the Heart stands out as an anomalous and barren geologic feature. Devoid of vegetation, it marks the mythical location of the origin of the Nimiipuu people.

A small white metal column pokes from the ground under a stand of tall cottonwood trees beside the Heart. Push a button on the column and the recorded voice of a Nez Perce elder tells the creation story of the Nimiipuu and other tribes that have lived in the region since long before the arrival of Europeans. The voice describes how Coyote, the Trickster, fooled the ravenous monster and freed all the animals at the dawn of the tribe's history.

About a mile east of the Heart of the Monster is a historic wooden church with a small but loyal—and mostly elderly—congregation. Behind the historic building are the gravesites of many well-known people from

Nez Perce history, including Ellenwoods, Georges, Axtells, and Corbetts. Chief Lawyer, the articulate young Nez Perce man who became a part of Nez Perce history, is also buried there. His gravestone reads:

CHIEF LAWYER
ABOUT 74 YRS OF AGE
DIED JAN. 3, 1875
IN 1855 & 1863 HE WAS PRESENT AT THE GOV.
TREATIES AT WALLA WALLA REP. THE NEZ PERCE
INDIANS AND WAS ELECTED SPOKESMAN FOR
THE INDIANS RESIDING ON THE RESERVATION
HE WAS THE FIRST ELDER OF THE 1ST. PRESB.
CHURCH OF KAMIAH.
HE MADE TWO TRIPS TO WASH. D.C.
THIS MONUMENT IS ERECTED BY HIS DIRECT DESCENDANTS.

Also buried there is the Reverend James Hayes, 1857–1928. "Pioneer Indian Missionary of Pacific States," his epitaph reads. "Ordained 1881. First Indian to receive Doctor of Divinity degree, Chairman Nez Perce camp meeting 1925, President of Talmaks from 1909 until his death. Earnest Evangelist, Devoted Pastor, Faithful Presbyter, Defender of the Faith, Beloved by All."

Suzzanne (Carlson) Penney, age sixty-seven, and Luke Penney, sixty-nine, attend the First Indian Presbyterian Church. They met during the early 1970s as teenagers while attending Upward Bound. Suzzanne is non-native, from the mining town of Wallace, Idaho. Luke is a Nez Perce from Kamiah. "It was culture shock for me at the time because Upward Bound was 80 percent Native American," said Suzzanne. "I went because I knew I could get college credits while I was in high school."[1]

After college, Suzzanne began teaching at the Coeur d'Alene Tribal School along with Chris (Mahoney) Meyer, who went on to serve as director of education for the Coeur d'Alene Tribe. For many years, Suzzanne and Luke taught together in Kellogg, she at the middle school and he at the grade school level. They also met with students once a week for tutoring sessions at the McDonald's in Wallace.

Today, Luke and Suzzanne are retired from long teaching careers. With three children and four grandchildren, they are part of an extended family that represents many elements in the diverse spectrum of traditions that make up Nez Perce society. Their family includes teachers, scientists, and son-in-law and tribal ethnographer Josiah Pinkham. From the end of her driveway in a comfortable neighborhood in Kamiah, Suzzanne points up to the high butte where Lewis and Clark's Corps of Discovery first emerged from the arduous Lolo Trail, hungry, tired, and in need of help.

The tribe takes care of its elders, explains Suzzanne, even stacking firewood for them each winter. In addition to raising their own children, Luke and Suzzanne have hosted several foster children in their home over the years. They credit Isabel Bond with getting them started on their careers as teachers.

"Isabel never turned a student away, but she also could put her foot down," recalled Suzzanne. "She found ways to help, including finding a place in her home, but she didn't do handouts. She would help in other ways, offer ways for them to exchange work for help. That is an example we have been able to follow with our kids. I have always called her for advice."[2]

On this particular Sunday, the Penneys attended a sermon at their church led by the Nez Perce Reverend Dr. Cecil Corbett. He described how the resurrection of Christ had been foreordained in the Book of Numbers. Following the sermon, Dr. Corbett's niece, Lydia Corbett, presented a slide show and talk based on two months she recently spent in Santa Cruz, Bolivia, where she joined a group of young evangelicals working to bring the Christian message to indigenous Quechua Indians. Lydia described some of the personal challenges she faced during her trip and how she resolved them with her fellow missionaries. She explained that, in order to spread the Gospel, she and her coworkers played music, held services, and reached out to the community using beaded, colored bracelets that served as a shorthand code for the story of Christianity:

> The black bead represents the belief that everyone sins, and that sin makes it impossible to have a relationship with God. The red bead symbolizes the blood of Jesus and the belief that faith in Jesus and his sacrificial death are necessary for the forgiveness of sins. The white bead stands for purity and the Christian teaching that once you put your faith in Jesus, your sins are forgiven and you are made pure. The blue bead represents water baptism, which is a way of outwardly expressing the inward change that has happened. The green bead is to help teach the need for continued growth in the faith. The gold bead represents the streets of heaven lined with gold.

The fact that the First Indian Presbyterian Church in Kamiah sends missionaries abroad to preach to indigenous congregations is a testament to the dedication of the Nez Perce ministers who were ordained there during the nineteenth century. Surely one reason Isabel's grandfather, the Reverend Daniel O'Connell Gamble, chose not to minister to the Nez Perce when he first arrived in Idaho was because Presbyterian missionaries had already been quite active in the area. As had many other Christian communities in the United States, the Nez Perce put their own stamp on the Christian faith.

THE VALUE OF CULTURAL FREEDOM

The Spaldings' mission in Nez Perce country was abandoned for a period, followed by a mission in Kamiah led by Kate and Sue McBeth, missionary sisters and teachers to the Nez Perce during the last quarter of the nineteenth century. During this tumultuous period, the McBeth sisters endeavored to bring education and the Christian message to the tribe.

Sue McBeth, a scholar and linguist, established a successful theological seminary for Nez Perce men, collected and organized a Nez Perce–English dictionary, and wrote abundantly about her experience. After her death in 1893, her younger sister Kate continued her work in literacy education and assumed responsibility for training Native American ministers.[3] Whereas the Spaldings had at times coerced the Nez Perce, the McBeths were more willing to appreciate the Native American language and customs. Nevertheless, they were prevented from attaining the rank of ministers themselves in a church that continued to limit the status of women.

"The McBeths allowed tribal members to dig camas roots, keep their hair long, and follow many traditions," said Luke. "This differed in this way from the early Spalding mission. Only one McBeth sister was in favor of the Dawes Act and of having an Indian agent."[4] The Dawes Act of 1877 served to reduce Nez Perce lands considerably during the era of assimilation by allotting parcels to individual members of the tribe and thereby allowing land sales to non-Indians.[5] The law was considered a disaster by many US tribes that lost millions of acres of tribal territory to land prospectors.

Luke still gathers medicinal and staple roots traditionally used by the Nez Perce, including camas root, which he and his family bake and store. As a kid, he drew water from a spring on the hill above the First Indian Presbyterian Church. Luke was raised by three aunts whose families had long been attached to the church. His grandmother had been adopted by one of the first ranchers in Idaho. "My aunties always wore moccasins," said Luke. "The only time they wore shoes was on Sundays. We didn't have running water, but we had the sweathouse to get clean in. The older generation didn't let us take sweats on Sundays, but we still do dawn sweats to honor deceased loved ones. Our church brought back the native culture that the Catholics had taken away. All day Friday was spent studying native culture."[6]

Penney said he does not depend upon church doctrine to live a spiritual life. "I like the saying, 'I will be a fisher of men.' God will speak to me in the wilds. That is the way we trained our kids. It doesn't depend upon the liturgy of the church. You just take care of your neighbors."[7]

The Penneys were married in 1971 and continued to work as dorm advisers and teachers at Upward Bound while attending the University of Idaho. "When things were tough, Isabel made sure we had a babysitter," said Suzzanne. "When we thought of dropping out of school, she made things happen so we could stay in school and get our degrees. We in turn have helped out at Upward Bound and recruited many students to the program."[8]

Isabel is godmother to Luke and Suzzanne's three grown children. Her house was a second home to them while their parents attended the University of Idaho. The Penneys' youngest children stayed with their parents in the dorms during the six-week summer programs, getting exposed at a young age to university life and a diversity of world views. Today they have both earned PhDs; D'Lisa Penney-Pinkham is the principal of Lapwai High School. Their son, Aaron Penney, manages the Nez Perce Tribal Hatchery.

The Upward Bound program provided reliable sustenance for families that sometimes had to choose between a fulfilling educational experience and working to make money for food. "When Isabel started us working for Upward Bound, we had three good meals a day," said Luke. "She brought in many basic things that had been missing in high school. She made sure her kids went to work in the kitchen or elsewhere on campus to make money while they were there. They did not have to choose between a summer job and an Upward Bound experience."[9]

Luke was tested by a speed-reading machine at Upward Bound, which flashed numbers and letters to measure his reading ability. He was good at math, eventually earning a degree in physical education plus elementary and secondary school teaching certificates. For three years, he taught at the Lapwai Elementary and High Schools. For ten more years, he taught at the Coeur d'Alene Tribal School. "I taught fourth through eighth grade, more math than anything else. When I first interviewed, I thought it was for a physical education position, but when they saw my credentials, they instead hired me as their full-time fourth-grade teacher."[10]

After her four years at Upward Bound during high school, Suzzanne earned a bachelor's degree in English and was aiming for a law degree.

"I interviewed at Coeur d'Alene Tribal School as a teacher's aide and wound up—because of Isabel's recommendation, I believe—walking out as a first grade teacher," she said.[11]

INSTILLING CULTURAL APPRECIATION

For the last seventeen years of his career, Luke worked as an elementary school teacher away from the tribe in the Kellogg School District. There he worked to get indigenous studies, dancing, and other customs into the mainstream school curriculum at Pinehurst Elementary School. "These were kids who had never been south of Coeur d'Alene. They had no idea there was an Indian reservation within a hundred miles of them."[12]

Luke looked at the school's curriculum and saw that it had only three chapters on Native Americans. He decided to get away from the book altogether and have students make folders with indigenous elements, including roots and other things they could touch and taste. "We brought in Coeur d'Alene elders to tell them stories. Pretty soon we had fourth-graders from several surrounding schools coming to Pinehurst to listen to them," he recalled.[13]

Luke then shared his ideas, contacts, and materials with other schools in the area, and brought in a dance and drumming group from the Coeur d'Alene Reservation to perform in the gymnasium. He dressed in traditional regalia to participate. "It brought down the house," Luke commented. "We had to do more native things with students, so we made Indian war shields. These were all non-native students. We would work on our war shields while listening to native music, both traditional and contemporary. One shield had deer antlers hanging from it. They did awesome work from just paint and cardboard."[14]

The war shields, each with individualized motifs, were displayed for one month at the Kellogg School District boardroom office. Luke then had his class study the Frank Church–River of No Return Wilderness. After familiarizing them with maps and readings on the area, he took a group of students on a jet boat trip up the Snake River Canyon, along with chaperones and parents who came along. They met at Hells Canyon

Creek boat launch at six in the morning. "We had been studying about Idaho history. Now they had to see Idaho's deepest canyon. We went to Pittsburg Landing, forty miles away, and returned that evening."[15]

The Native American classes were so successful that Luke decided to involve some of his Indian relatives and friends. The staff and family members of Pinehurst Elementary were by now quite enthusiastic about learning native traditions. They held fundraising events for weeks to pay to send their kids to Nez Perce country. Luke was able to call on his own rich tradition to expand the public school curriculum, allowing for a cultural exchange that left a lasting impression on his students. "I took them on an overnight field trip to Lapwai, where my cousin was a school principal. The kids had a blast there, learning how to set up a tipi and going through the museum. They had never seen Lewiston before, and they were amazed. They all took pictures of how deep the canyon was. All they could talk about was the great potential for sledding on the hills of the Palouse. Then they smelled the Potlatch Mill, and they were all gasping for breath."[16]

Luke took the group on a guided tour of the tribe's administrative headquarters and surrounding neighborhoods. "We walked up to my nephew's place and had Indian tacos, sixty kids and adults in a small restaurant. At seven o'clock Mike Penney had his drum group come for a mini powwow. Isabel found out about what we were doing and found resources to repeat the experience for other schools."[17]

About twenty miles from Lapwai, the first Teton wolves had been brought from Wyoming to Winchester, Idaho, on the Nez Perce Reservation. This is where the tribe worked with the federal government on the state's first gray wolf reintroduction project at a time when the state refused to participate. For many years, buffalo hunters and then stockmen had hunted wolves to the point of extinction in the United States. The tribe took on the task of helping reintroduce them to the wild, keeping them temporarily in large pens on reservation land.[18] Luke brought two fourth-grade classes to see them. "They had to be very quiet so they could actually see a real live wolf," he recalled.[19]

Suzzanne was providing similar cultural experiences for her students in the Kellogg Middle School during the 1990s, setting up education stations to show kids about the mines in the area where they grew up. She also became a primary fundraiser for this educational program.

While Luke and Suzzanne were following Isabel Bond's example of incorporating cultural elements into lessons and working as teachers and curriculum developers at Idaho grade schools, Isabel and her staff were bringing the next generation of students through the Upward Bound program. Educational equity had improved since the earliest days of Upward Bound, and by now a growing trend toward multiculturalism, along with increasing respect for individual ethnic groups, was widely apparent at colleges and universities across the country. Yet it remained a struggle in northern Idaho to locate and recruit students from rural areas, and Upward Bound staff faced challenges in keeping students in the program once they were enrolled.

Chapter 11

◈ IN TWO WORLDS ◈

NATIVE AMERICAN and mainstream communities often hold different cultural and historical perspectives on the same region. Upward Bound drew together young people from both worlds in ways that transformed their lives forever. Forty-four-year-old Mary Taylor grew up in Grangeville, a city of about three thousand near the southernmost end of the Nez Perce Reservation. Mary, who is non-Indian, followed her older sister into the program in 1989. She joined Upward Bound initially to escape an uncomfortable family situation with her father and stepmother. "After I got there, I realized that what I was learning was very positive. This was a time when people could discover for themselves who they liked and what they thought, a time of self-realization and growing up."[1]

Mary grew up a short distance from White Bird Grade, a hill that descends steeply to the Salmon River and past the site of the first major battle of the 1877 Nez Perce War. Like so many people on the reservation, Mary was exposed to two different world views growing up. "I usually get along better with natives than white people," said Mary, who is now a dental assistant after working at the Coeur d'Alene Casino for ten years. "I have always liked certain aspects of their culture, like how they take care of their families, how a stranger can become a part of the family and be taken in and shown how things are done."[2]

Isabel at Selway campground with confiscated bottle rockets, 1993.
Private collection. Photograph by Darlene Dyer.

Upward Bound classes were challenging for Mary, who joined sixty other students on campus in the dorms. It did not take long for some of them to drop out. "It was an intense program," she said. "You had to get up early, you had to go to school, and you had to be responsible for maintaining yourself. You gained a sense of personal responsibility and personal management. I was rebellious and didn't care about school, but working with Upward Bound teachers who helped with study skills made a difference. Without Isabel and her program, I would not have graduated from high school. The teachers were inspirational, and Isabel was easy to talk to if you had any problems. She was not one of those directors who you heard about but never saw. She came down the river on the raft with us and helped kids set up their tents. Those were great summers."[3]

Mary enjoyed the educational field trips, weekend camping, river rafting, and a summer horse program in which the students rode horses that were stabled on campus. Upward Bound staff had received permission from the U of I School of Agriculture to use their corral and horse barn for afternoon horse classes. Students used Isabel's or Darlene's horses, or in some cases brought their own to campus. Isabel employed a woman from California who specialized in therapeutic riding. The theme for that year was "Summer of the Horse." For six weeks, each student was engaged in some aspect of caring for horses. Equestrian studies were incorporated into study skills, math, science, and English classes. Students went to WSU's College of Veterinary Medicine to learn more about equestrian medicine.

"Some of us had never been around horses, so this was our first exposure to them," said Mary. "We learned how to saddle and bridle and care for our horses. We got to ride every day." She appreciated the fact that there were no cliques at Upward Bound, no popular kids, or bad kids, cool kids, or nerds:

> There were no preset conditions. Students who came from the same school and did not get along there would all get along at Upward Bound. It was a level playing field with no influences from the outside world. We had to rely on each other for help with homework. Not everyone gets a six-week period of new experiences to discover for themselves what is right and wrong.
>
> I had been picked on at my school for not hanging out with the right group, but at Upward Bound, no one felt like a stranger. Former students came back to work as staff and took us under their wings. This made it easy to learn and get along with everybody.[4]

Mary moved from Grangeville to attend North Idaho College in Coeur d'Alene. After graduating, she worked at the Coeur d'Alene Casino. "I enjoyed my job at the casino, and my coworkers," she said, but she decided to make a change in 2012, enrolling in the Carrington College in California in hope of starting a new career as a dental assistant. Skills she had learned many years before at Upward Bound served her well, including the Cornell University note-taking method. "You make a line down one third of the page, take notes on one side of the line, and write down questions on the other side."[5]

Mary graduated the accelerated two-year program in ten months and has now worked for one year in a new job. "I am working in a great place with excellent people," she said. Now she lives in Post Falls with her son. She is Facebook friends with many of her former Upward Bound classmates and is regularly in touch with Isabel. "She has always helped me out if she could. She even comes to my son's birthday parties when she has the time and is able."[6]

CULTURAL CROSSCURRENTS

Although kids of a certain age have many things in common, the layers of history in Idaho offer diverse perspectives to students from differing backgrounds. Mabel "Robin" Black Eagle, also forty-four, is descended from the Wallowa band of Chief Joseph and his brother Ollokot. Her father, Martin Black Eagle, is descended from Reuben Black Eagle, a spiritual healer. These days, Mabel works as a community coordinator aide at the Wa-A'Yas Community Center in Kamiah. "I come from a family that is spread across the entire Nez Perce Reservation. My father tells me that I am related to everyone in the tribe even though I married a white man," she said.[7]

Yolanda Guzman Bisbee was one of Mabel's Upward Bound counselors, along with Phillip Allen. Having these Native American counselors made it easier for Mabel to fit in on campus because they understood where she was from. But in 1992, Mabel was failing in her grades during her sophomore year in high school and was told she had to finish her classes with passing grades or be held back a year.

"I was pretty good at science and math, but not at all with English, writing, and reading," Mabel recalled. "I had some older cousins who attended Upward Bound. They were there almost every year because they loved the place. Kamiah was small. I was a small-town girl who had gone to the same building for elementary school and middle school. When I went to Upward Bound at the U of I campus, there were huge, beautiful lawns and trees and tall buildings, each one offering something different. I struggled the first week remembering where I had to go. It seems like I wound up in the wrong classroom once or twice."[8]

During her first week at Upward Bound, Mabel's older cousins encouraged her to bully another student who they said did not fit in with their group. "She wanted to hang out with us, but she dressed up in these tight pants and cowgirl boots. Well, my cousins would rather dress up in the '80s style with big hair. They just didn't want this girl standing around with us. My cousins knew I was an easy target. I let peer pressure get to me and listened to older kids tell me to pick on this younger girl."[9]

What Mabel did not realize at the time was that Isabel and her staff had carefully cultivated an atmosphere at Upward Bound where students could interact without the usual social pressures of high school. Mabel told the younger girl not to sit by them, but Isabel was watching, and she came over and took Mabel aside for a talk. "She said she did not approve of that kind of action, so she was sending me home. The truth is that I was happy to go because I did not want to spend my summer in school away from fishing and camping."

Mabel's father, Martin Black Eagle, arrived on campus to take her back to Kamiah. He gave her a long speech during the two-hour ride home. "He read me the riot act about how important education is. He said we all had to make sacrifices from our usual freedoms. By the time I got to Kamiah, it was pretty well decided that I was going back and that I would have to sincerely apologize to Isabel."[10]

Mabel was reminded by her father about a time in her family's history when education in some of the white man's ways became vital for the tribe. "I grew up going to church in Kamiah, but I knew that other sides of my family had followed more of the Dreamer religion. My dad had told us about when scarlet fever and the pox came along. The traditional healers tried but could not help. He said his grandmother was still doing medicine dances to heal people, but some of them died and the families got mad at her for not helping."[11]

By the time her father was ready to drop her off in Kamiah, Mabel had reconsidered the importance of higher education. Somehow, Isabel was also there. "She was doing something nearby with some horses when we arrived," Mabel said. "I don't know if she had planned this with my father, but I had to get right in her face and apologize. She was watching me closely to see how sincere I was. Isabel agreed to take me back to the university as long as I didn't pull any more of my shenanigans. I have only good things to say about Mrs. Isabel Bond today. She wouldn't let me fail. Although she temporarily expelled me from Upward Bound for bullying, her intention was to teach me a lesson of respect."[12]

Mabel gained a new perspective on her homeland later that summer when a group of students were brought to the Pullman-Moscow Airport for a private flight in a small airplane. "The flight instructor took off, and we flew over the reservation. He let me push in the throttle and push on the pedals and steer, to see what it was like to fly an airplane," said Mabel.[13] She looked down for the first time on Nez Perce country and the surrounding Palouse region of rolling hills that give way to deep gorges along the Clearwater and Salmon Rivers. They flew toward the vast Camas Prairie, across many square miles of farmland, and high above Kamiah. She could see the dense Nez Perce National Forest and mountains back behind Kamiah where the tribe had once migrated along the Lolo Trail to Montana for buffalo hunting.

The plane flew farther south toward Grangeville, beyond which the prairie drops off into White Bird Grade and then descends toward the deep valley of the Salmon River. The plane then looped back toward Lewiston above the Nez Perce Reservation's western boundary, flying above Cottonwood and Winchester and then back to the airport for a landing. "It took no more than twenty minutes, and we were able to see pretty much the whole reservation," Mabel recalled.[14]

Despite the positive experience at Upward Bound, Mabel dropped out of high school the year she was supposed to graduate. By that time, she had taken out a car loan to buy a Ford Bronco and had to come up with the payments. "They were paying twenty-five dollars an hour to work at a road construction site, so I dropped out of school to go flag traffic." For twelve more years, Mabel made a living at flagging, but she also stayed in touch with Isabel. In 2008, Mabel decided to return to her studies. "I finished my GED because I wanted to do more with my life than road construction."[15]

The GED diploma got Mabel into college with Phillip Allen at the Northwest Indian College in Lapwai, where she took general education requirements with an emphasis on Native American culture and literature. She studied in-depth the natural environment she had flown over years before at Upward Bound, the land where her ancestors had lived for thousands of years. "I have been told that studying in Lapwai is totally different than a mainstream college. It brought to life things I thought I knew about but didn't. It opened my eyes to what our people struggled through. I learned what our treaties mean to us. I learned that what we were promised by the federal government is different than what we were given," she said.[16]

Mabel attended a class offered by Phil Allen about the shifting history of the tribe's relationship with the US government, leading up to the Indian Reorganization Act of 1934, which marked a return to tribal self-governance after many years of assimilation policies and put an end to the Dawes allotment era.[17] Tribes then fought for and eventually won passage of the Indian Civil Rights Act of 1968, which provided most of the same civil rights other American citizens enjoyed, including protection from unjust tribal authorities.

Mabel learned how self-determination was further bolstered by passage of the Indian Self-Determination and Education Assistance Act of 1975, which ended generations of paternalism by the federal government and authorized government agencies to enter into contracts with, and make grants directly to, federally recognized Indian tribes. Native

Americans now had the chance to take control of their own education, bringing Native American languages, beliefs, and philosophies into the classroom.[18]

Thanks to the Native American-specific curriculum offered in Lapwai, Mabel gained a new perspective on her people's relations with the federal government and her tribe's obligations to its members. "These laws created our tribal government, but our tribal council is only a government branch. They are not the treaty holders. The treaty is for us as individuals, for our rights, our health care, our education, and our homes. I hate to say it, but these promises are not always being lived up to." Eventually, Mabel received an associate's degree and bachelor's degrees in science and native environmental science. "It was a lot of work, but the time went by so fast. It was a lot of fun and I wish it had never ended. Isabel visited with me some years ago, and we talked about these things when I was trying to work on a Nez Perce tribal cooperative for storing, freezing, and canning fish near Riggins."[19]

After Mabel found that she could not get help from the tribe because the operation was required to be on the reservation, she went to the BIA. That also did not pan out, so Isabel encouraged her to apply to the state's Clearwater Economic Development Association for a grant. Because she was planning to create a for-profit business, Mabel ran into yet more roadblocks. "In any case, Isabel has followed along with me and tried in every way she can to help me get my business going," Mabel said.[20]

NON-INDIAN ACCULTURATION

Even as many Native American students used their education to navigate the non-Indian world, some non-Indian Upward Bound students found purpose and meaning in the Native American cultures they encountered. This process of acculturation is reflected in the story of Chelle-Rene (Merrill) Josefowicz.

The airplane flight Mabel took in 1992 would have passed over a wooded area on the outskirts of the reservation boundary and the remote village called Forest, Idaho, where Chelle lived as a child. She grew up living in a tent with no running water, electricity, or TV. "My parents were hippies, very anti-government," said Chelle, now fifty-one and retired from a military career. "There was a lot of drinking and drugs. We lived like it was the 1800s. Do you know how cold it gets in a tent in Forest, Idaho, in the winter? I didn't have much of a family history of my own. There were no pictures of me as a kid. I think my mother was bipolar. My father was alcoholic, and so he had a hard time keeping a job."[21]

Chelle attended Craigmont High School, but because of her living circumstances, she had few friends until she transferred to Lapwai High School. There she met a Nez Perce girl named April Williams. "I would never have survived if I had not been taken in by April and her family. I was pretty self-destructive. I certainly would not have graduated high school if not for Upward Bound."[22] Chelle said goodbye to her parents after her junior year and moved to the Nez Perce Reservation. She and April were Lapwai cheerleaders and attended Upward Bound together. "Moving to Lapwai was like winning the lottery for me. I was called the token white girl. They called me Dopey because I was always so goofy. The fact is, I would not be here today if it were not for Upward Bound and the families and counselors at Lapwai."[23]

Chelle became a part of April's extended family. She met the Watters family, including Upward Bound cultural liaison Mari Watters and her nephew, O.J. Watters. Mari gave Chelle her first Appaloosa horse and named it Gypsy-Cochise, after the Chiricahua Apache chief Cochise. "She also taught me how to do beadwork and make shawls and how to speak some of the Nez Perce language. These people taught me about family, how to take care of one another, and how to take care of ourselves. They were also there to make sure we graduated from high school."[24]

Chelle watched movies for the first time on a VCR at Peggy Two-Hatchet's house. She braided O.J. Watters' hair in history class. "O.J. was kind of a trickster. When we went to Wallowa Lake on the Upward Bound trip, he took me snipe hunting. I didn't know any better. He teased me, told me to call out for the snipes but to not whistle, because if I whistled the

Stick Indians would come after me. These were some kind of spirits that lived in the lake. I was terrified."[25]

Chelle went to powwows and attended pipe ceremonies and Seven Drum honoring ceremonies. April's father showed Chelle how to smoke salmon and make jerky from buffalo that the family hunted in Montana. During the summer, they went together to the Yakama powwow and to Crow Agency in Montana for the massive annual Crow Fair and Sun Dances.

Chelle furthered her interest in Native American religions and later in Buddhism. During her senior year, she attended the Bridge program to prepare for college. After graduation, she joined the US Navy as a religion program specialist. The job was a fulfillment of interests from her youth. "My parents hated religion so there had never been an opportunity to pursue my spiritual interests," she said.[26] After a wide-ranging career as a paramedic and firefighter, Chelle Merrill Josefowicz has three grown children and is retired, living near Huntsville, Alabama. Her work has involved providing disaster relief, body recovery, and counseling at Ground Zero in Manhattan following the 9/11 attacks, and similar work after major hurricanes and floods.

Chelle said that the time she spent among the Nez Perce in her youth had a lasting effect on her life and career. She memorized the famous speech Chief Joseph gave during his surrender at the Bear Paw Battlefield in 1877, reciting it as part of one of her college history class requirements. "I made sure my three children know a lot about the Nez Perce. I have told them stories about Idaho all of their lives," Chelle said.[27]

Chelle had not spoken to her father in twenty years when she located him in 2010. "He was always a white-water guy, so we took a rafting trip down the Salmon River to the old native rock paintings near China Hole. It takes three days to get there by boat. I don't know if there is any other way to get there. We talked about many things on the trip. It was good therapy."[28]

Since retiring recently, Chelle continues to volunteer abroad. Thanks to her childhood experiences, she found that she could survive with few comforts. Recently, she traveled with an aid group to help tribes in the Maasai Mara of Kenya. "It may have been a struggle for some of them, but for me it was easy. One of our native drivers and supply guides wanted to hear my stories about the natives in America. I told him about living in Lapwai and how the families there were very similar to the Maasai. They honored their elders and shared everything."[29]

MAINSTREAM SOCIETY THROUGH A NEZ PERCE LENS

Having access to one's Native American traditions can bring a lifelong shift in perspective. Like dental hygienist Mary Taylor, Jenny Albert Blackeagle also grew up in the town of Grangeville, a place known as Sike Sike in the Nez Perce language. Grangeville is located on the edge of the vast Camas Prairie, which since time immemorial has been an important foraging and meeting place for tribes. Gold miners poured into this area in the 1860s, setting the stage for a conflict that led to the rout of US troops by Nez Perce warriors in 1877 during the Battle of White Bird Canyon.

Although Jenny was a Nez Perce tribal member, she grew up knowing little about her Native American heritage. But her mother, Kathy Blackeagle, always encouraged her to attain a college education. Her cousins and her sisters Beverly and Daisy had attended Upward Bound before her, so when Jenny was fourteen, she was enrolled in the program and traveled to the U of I campus. "Upward Bound was very tough because I had never been away from home, alone," said Jenny. "I had never been away from my mother. I would get so homesick."[30]

Isabel went to great lengths to encourage Jenny to complete the program, but to no avail. "I think now about the opportunity she was presenting, and I regret that I did not take it," she said. Many years later, Jenny enrolled in classes at the Northwest Indian College campus in Lapwai, studying under Phil Allen and others. She furthered her passion for Native American studies during one year of classes at the University of Idaho. "Isabel put me up in her house for a week when I was going to U of I. She asked what I needed. I have the utmost honor and respect for her. I didn't know it at the time, but as an adult I do.

Isabel shined a light on education for the Nez Perce people. We need many more Isabel Bonds."[31]

Jenny, now forty-six, is part of a new generation of Native American students poised to make positive and lasting changes for the tribe. Today, she works at the Nez Perce National Historical Park in the Pathways Internship Program. The program was designed for native and non-native college students to provide job opportunities and extensive state-of-the-art research materials about the Nez Perce National Historic Trail across Washington, Idaho, Oregon, and Montana.

Like many former Upward Bound students, Jenny continues to set her sights on future academic goals. "I am currently enrolled at University of California Los Angeles for online Native Law classes. My ultimate goal is to get a law degree, but right now I am working for the one-year tribal law certificate. I picked UCLA because Carole Goldberg, a renowned Native Law professor, taught there. My passion is to study tribal law for the defense of my tribal members." Jenny said her studies began as a hobby. "But then I would stay awake reading more and more when I began to learn about the injustices against my people. I thought I might as well go to school."[32]

Under Professor Phil Allen at the Northwest Indian College in Lapwai, Jenny studied sovereignty issues, treaties, federal trust obligations, and hunting and fishing rights. She noted, "I was raised off the reservation, so I had very vague knowledge about my culture and my history. Phil's classes have empowered me in many ways. I know now that my ancestors thought of the Seven Generations down the line. When they signed the treaty of 1855, they thought about us living now. They gave us all the tools we need, but it is up to each individual to decipher them and use them accordingly, the way our ancestors wanted us to."[33]

Jenny was further inspired by the tribal law classes she took for her minor in Native American studies at the University of Idaho College of Law, taught by Professor Angelique Townsend EagleWoman, who served as general counsel to her tribe, the Sisseton Wahpeton Oyate of the Lake Traverse Reservation, and as a public defender for two tribes in Oklahoma. Jenny said:

> It is all about education. If you have studied enough your own treaties, you can have a higher level of knowledge and understanding of the legal document. Our ancestors never wanted us to be prosecuted or overrun by non-tribal members. They already knew the government was not to be trusted because they had been driven off their lands and killed by the US Army.
>
> Each tribe has a different set of circumstances, but poverty, drugs, and alcohol problems are always a part of them. I have economic dreams for our tribe. Not everyone understands our history and tribal laws or our community services.[34]

Jenny noted that the Intercourse and Trade Act is a good place to begin. "This law lets only the US government interact with us, but it does not mean we cannot interact economically and legally with other tribes in business relationships. We historically had a very large trading area and traveled all across what is now called the USA. We were neither stagnant nor nomadic. My ancestors traveled with purpose and were knowledgeable experts on how to survive."

In 2007, Jenny's three-year-old son was diagnosed with severe autism. One year later, another son was diagnosed with attention deficit disorder. "My son would stay up until four in the morning because the cable TV at grandpa's house never stopped. There was a constant flow of information. I knew I had to change their lives for the better or they would be dependent the rest of their lives."[35]

Jenny's renewed interest in Nez Perce traditions has given her a new perspective on mainstream society. Several years ago, she took her family a step away from mainstream American consumer society. The Albert family has no cable TV, newspapers, and no department store advertising in their home. "It changed my lifestyle as well," she said. "We watch DVDs and have Internet access, but we don't watch TV shows or listen to the radio anymore. We read. We study a lot.

There is more family time. My kids think for themselves more and more. My son now has more communication skills. We try to do a lot of traditional things. We just returned from our first traditional fishing trip and were very successful."[36]

Chapter 12

EXPANDING INFLUENCE

ABOUT FIFTEEN years ago, Isabel Bond and Upward Bound teacher Darlene Dyer were driving through a light drizzle on a back road in Lapwai when Isabel pointed out a small herd of horses standing at a distance across a field. Isabel stopped the car and walked across the field to the herd, recognizing one two-year-old colt in particular.

"They were just hanging out together under a huge tree in this barren pasture," said Darlene. "All of the horses walked or ran away, except for the colt that stood there looking at Isabel. The horse was obviously glad to see her and walked up to Isabel's hand. Isabel told me that day that if you are there at a horse's birth, it will never forget you."[1]

RETURN TO HORSE CULTURE

Isabel had helped birth the Appaloosa colt at the Gamble farm below Paradise Ridge. The colt was then brought into the Nez Perce Horse Registry program Isabel had helped establish. A Navajo named Rudy Shebala and his Native American protégés were raising the horses, reinvigorating a practice that rested deep in Nez Perce tribal tradition.

During the mid 1990s, Isabel and others collaborated on a plan to develop a new breed called "the Nez Perce Horse," with plans to market them as a source of economic development. The resulting Nez Perce Horse Registry initiated the launch of a new breeding strain using western Appaloosa mares and four rare Akhal-Teke stallions from Turkmenistan in Central Asia. Researchers discovered that the small herds found there were the ancestral stock of horses the Nez Perce obtained from early Russian fur trappers in the Northwest. The Akhal-Teke/Appaloosa cross combined characteristics of this sturdy Asian breed with a breed made famous by the Nez Perce before Lewis and Clark arrived in Idaho.[2] Meriwether Lewis noted in a February 15, 1806, journal entry that the Nez Perce Appaloosas "appear to be of an excellent race; they are lofty, elegantly formed, active and durable; in short many of them look like fine English corsers [*sic*] and would make a figure in any country."[3]

The horse registry program, Mounted Scholars, and Young Horsemen Project helped reconnect young members of the tribe to equestrian knowledge that had once been central to Nez Perce culture.[4] Isabel's passion for horses again coincided with her work as an educator when a rancher named Bob Browning from Farmington, New Mexico, contacted the Nez Perce Tribe. "He said he was frustrated because he could find nothing to read about the tribe that had taken place since the end of the war of 1877," said Lucinda George, who by that time was working in law enforcement, married to Nez Perce tribal chairman Allen Pinkham Sr., and working as a drug and alcohol counselor. "Bob said he knew the tribe had been famous for breeding Appaloosa horses. He said he had twenty-five registered Appaloosas for us if we wanted them. I just knew that we could use these horses to help our young people," she said.[5]

Lucinda went to work, writing a three-page paper to Browning that explained what the Nez Perce Tribe planned to do with the horses. "I described how we would engage our youth in cultural and traditional horse activities to lessen drug and alcohol dependence." Two weeks later, Browning came to Lapwai and stayed with Lucinda and Allen. "Al said we could keep the horses to begin with on land he owned near Lenore," said Lucinda. "Isabel then helped write the constitution and bylaws for the Chief Joseph Foundation, which was established to facilitate the Mounted Scholars program."[6]

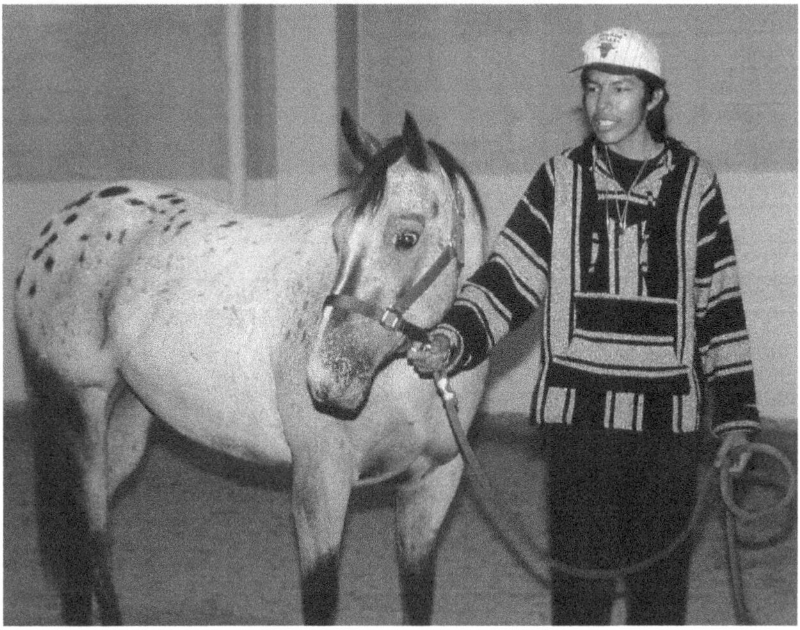

Upward Bound student Isaac Broncheau walking Matt's Mare, 1993.
Private collection. Photograph by Darlene Dyer.

Isabel then went to work writing a grant application to the Kellogg Foundation that would eventually fund the Mounted Scholars. This after-school program would serve to help children from middle school to high school age that were doing poorly in school because of issues at home. By providing the opportunity to spend time with horses, the Mounted Scholars, based in Lapwai, rewarded students who kept their grades up and attended a study hall. Eventually, the students would learn to care for horses, become skilled riders, and continue the legacy of horsemanship the Nez Perce Tribe had been famous for in generations past.

Lucinda followed Isabel's lead by writing a second grant for the Mounted Scholars, employing her master's thesis from Eastern Washington University to obtain another grant from the Kellogg Foundation. On November 3, 1996, the *New York Times* reported on the success of the program: "Math, history, and other subjects are taught, with the curriculum built around horses. Classes include riding instruction."[7]

"The outside of a horse," said Rosa Yearout, a board member of the program, "helps the inside of a kid." The pride generated by the horses on a reservation beset with high unemployment and other social ills is almost palpable. "His name is Skeeter, and he's my little horse, 'cause I always ride him," said one twelve-year-old girl in the Mounted Scholars program, as she sat on an Appaloosa. Children are taught about Jackson Sundown, the nephew of Chief Joseph, who was the saddle bronc champion at the Pendleton Round-Up in 1916. With his braids tied together under his chin, the fifty-year-old Nez Perce rode a horse name Angel to victory.[8]

Major donors to the Chief Joseph Foundation have included the Richard Gere Foundation, Tom Redman, the Meyer Memorial Trust, and The Disney Foundation.[9] Lilian Disney, the widow of Walt Disney, grew up in Lapwai. Her father had worked on the reservation for the US government as a blacksmith and federal marshal. One year before she passed away in 1997, at age ninety-eight, she donated $100,000 to the Nez Perce Tribe when they were seeking to buy some ancient tribal artifacts.[10]

Each year, the Chief Joseph Foundation raises money to send up to five Nez Perce youths on the National Chief Joseph Trail Ride, which follows the trail the Nez Perce used to flee from the US Cavalry during the 1877 war. Young riders learn firsthand about the arduous 1,170-mile trek that Chiefs Joseph, Looking Glass, White Bird, Ollokot, Lean Elk, and others undertook with nearly 750 Nez Perce men, women, and children and twice that number of horses through the mountains to Montana on the Lolo Trail.

This historic route, which was only used once in its entirety—and then only in desperation—connects many of the sites visited by the Upward Bound students on their 1988 Chief Joseph Trail trip to the Big Hole Battlefield. Modern-day riders undertake the route in stages only, starting at Wallowa Lake in Oregon, heading northeast, and across the Snake River at Dug Bar. The riders then enter Idaho at Lewiston and cut across north-central Idaho, entering Montana near Lolo Pass. After traveling through the Bitterroot Valley, they reenter Idaho at Bannock Pass and travel east back into Montana at Targhee Pass to cross the Continental Divide.[11] The ride bisects Yellowstone National Park and then follows the Clarks Fork of the Yellowstone River out of Wyoming into Montana and north to the Bear Paw Mountains, ending forty miles from the Canadian border. Chief Joseph and his followers trekked the entire route from June to October 1877. Today, riders take thirteen years to complete the route in one-hundred-mile stages. Nevertheless, they are inspired by the journey. "Best ride ever and a great opportunity in sharing the history of the trail," said a young rider named Katherine, a National Chief Joseph Trail Ride youth sponsored by the Chief Joseph Foundation, as posted on the foundation's website. "It made me very proud of my heritage and I liked sharing my culture with other riders. I enjoyed meeting so many different people and making new friends."[12]

Nikoli, another youth rider sponsored by the Chief Joseph Foundation, said the ride was "very heartbreaking because of the past history the trail holds. Following our ancestors' tracks made me realize the hardships our people went through. I also felt a deep sense of pride in being Nez Perce and sharing native songs and stories with other riders."[13]

The Chief Joseph Foundation partners with the Nez Perce Tribal Health Authority, Special Olympics Idaho, the Lapwai Boys and Girls Clubs, the Lapwai School District, and the Department of Animal and Veterinarian Science at the University of Idaho. For many years, Isabel sought to further expand the program, relying on qualified and dedicated staff to fulfill federal requirements and find new opportunities for grants and collaborations. Having honed her understanding of grant-writing details over many years, she often took on the role of training conference attendees in effective grant-writing techniques.

LIFTING UPWARD BOUND STAFF

Isabel could not have succeeded without dedicated staff members like Connie Fleener, who stuck by her side for many years. Connie worked for Isabel for seventeen years as a counselor, office assistant, budget technician, associate director, and finally as director of the Talent Search program Isabel helped establish at U of I.

"Isabel and I were writing a lot of grants," said Connie. "I could read her handwriting because I had been around her for so many years. Her husband John would then critique the grants. Isabel and I have shared disappointments, joys, graduations, weddings, births, and deaths. I believe I am the person I am today due to the influence she had on my life."[14]

Connie, age fifty-eight, whose two grown children are both college students, grew up in Kellogg, Idaho, when it was a thriving mining town. "My story is not much different than other Upward Bound students needing a guiding hand. My dad worked as a truck driver for Bunker Hill Mine, and Mom took care of her five children. Because we were low-income, first-generation college families, Isabel accepted us. I have two brothers and two sisters. Every single one of us went to Upward Bound."[15]

Connie credits a strong family support system for her and her siblings' success, especially after the mining industry collapsed. "Dad and Mom and all my sisters and brothers attended each other's activities. We did a lot of camping and fishing and attended church every Sunday. We took road trips together. My older sister, Tammy, was recruited to attend this summer program called Upward Bound at the University of Idaho to help her with her grades. I was upset that she was accepted first because I had better grades than her. I knew someday, somehow, I would also attend college. Kellogg was almost entirely white. We had only one Hispanic family, and the daughter from that family also came with us to Upward Bound."[16]

Connie attended Upward Bound during the summers of 1975 and 1976, making friends that have lasted a lifetime, including Yolanda Guzman Bisbee, Bill Picard, Phil Allen, Shirley Allman, and Dean Pakotas. "Upward Bound had more Native Americans than whites. It took probably the first week for most students to feel we were all one big family. The Native American kids came to campus with this way of saying 'aaaay' to everything. By the end of a session they would have all of us saying 'aaaay,' and everyone else on campus was saying it too."[17]

Isabel and her staff, including Connie, wrote and administered the Minority High School Student Research Apprentice Program grant from 1978 to 1990. They implemented similar practices into Upward Bound to give young people a real sense of what it takes to work in a chosen occupation, putting students together with computer programmers or science professors to see if they enjoyed the field of study. "Anything you were interested in, Isabel would find a way to make an opportunity for you. You could job-shadow for a day with someone in the medical field or veterinary sciences. Of course, just to be on a big campus was something you thought you might never have experienced without Upward Bound."[18]

During her free time, Connie played racquetball, learned archery, and went on weekend camping trips. In her junior and senior years, she worked at the medical clinic in Kellogg, preparing patients for appointments, and attending to billing and scheduling. After graduating from high school in 1978, and with Upward Bound's assistance, she applied for and received financial aid and gained admission to North Idaho College in Coeur d'Alene. "It was a dream come true. I was the first person in my family to attend college. Yet, somehow just before graduation, I was informed that the government course I passed was not the one I needed to complete my associate's degree. Isabel came to the rescue. She hired me to be an Upward Bound counselor, living in the girl's dormitory while I took a government course to complete my degree."[19]

Connie graduated in August 1980 and went to Spokane to work for the *Spokesman-Review* and *Chronicle*, doing layout and graphics. She had studied legal secretarial science and worked for Idaho Legal Aid Services for a while before going back to U of I to complete her college education, so Isabel asked her if she wanted to apply for Upward Bound's secretarial position. She took the job. "While I was employed, Isabel encouraged me to take courses part-time. It took another nine years, but I finally received my bachelor's degree in 1989, and received the

'Outstanding Senior' award for the College of Education."[20]

The federal TRIO programs, which Upward Bound is a part of, also include the Talent Search and Student Support Services programs. The five-year Upward Bound grant application to the US Department of Education required student and family needs assessments in target areas, histories of mining towns and Indian reservations, data on income and educational levels, as well as plans for specific programs each summer. Connie Fleener helped write the grant each year and then tracked its progress, counting the number of meals served and rooms used for accommodations. She also evaluated class schedules.

No year at Upward Bound was the same as another. "One year, kids would be running around smoking pot or drinking and getting kicked out for spending the night in the wrong dorm. The next year, everything would go smoothly, and everyone was well-behaved. Isabel would kick them out, but she would also bring them back. The teachers would sometimes be mad because they thought some students had already been given enough chances. You don't always see success right away with these kids. Sometimes you would see it only five years later."[21]

In 1997, Fleener left the Upward Bound program to become a stay-at-home mom while her husband was out of state working for a helicopter logging company. Unfortunately the company went bankrupt, and her husband returned to Moscow. She was then hired as a branch office administrator for Edward Jones Investments in March 1998 and is still employed there today. "Both my sons have earned college degrees. Upward Bound's ultimate goal was accomplished. The chain of low-income kids without college educations has ended."[22]

PLANTING SEEDS OF POSSIBILITY

Isabel's influence continued to grow. She and her staff supported the Nez Perce Language Program and a vocational education program for the Nez Perce Tribe. She served on the Northwest Indian Youth Conference advisory board and worked with the University of Idaho's Native American Student Center as a faculty advisor. From 1980 to

2003, Isabel and her staff wrote and administered the grant for Helping Orient Indian Students and Teachers to Math and Science (HOIST) and served as a faculty advisor for the American Indian Science and Engineering Society (AISES). Isabel attended conferences such as these to discuss the particular challenges Native American kids faced when studying the sciences, made presentations on behalf of students in her region, and apprised conferees of strategies to improve the skills of high-risk students.

AISES works to integrate the cultural priorities and worldviews of Indian students with the demands of a scientific education. In 1994, Isabel traveled to an AISES conference in Boulder, Colorado, titled "Educating American Indian and Alaska Native Elementary and Secondary Students." Funded by the National Science Foundation, the conference brought Native American teachers and tribal advisers together with non-Indian teachers and administrators for a weekend-long exploration of ideas and possibilities. The words of Vine Deloria Jr., a Native American scholar and intellectual, were quoted in the conference catalog:

> In contrast to the predominantly mechanistic approach of Western science, the Indian view is "holistic in that it tries to present a comprehensive picture in which parts and their values are less significant than the larger picture and its meaning." American Indian cultures do not accept the separation of science from other aspects of life, yet Indian students are presented with a curriculum in which "knowledge of the world is divided up into separate categories that seem to be completely isolated from one another."
>
> Expressions of a science thought process abound throughout traditional American Indian agriculture, astronomy, ecology and medical practices. In addition, processes of science that include rational observation of natural events, classification and problem solving are woven into all aspects of American Indian culture. Despite this intricate knowledge of the natural world, American Indian culture and traditions are often not included in curricula. While mathematics

was used in sophisticated ways by many ancient tribal cultures, only Western mathematics history is treated in the classroom.[23]

By the early 2000s, the TRIO programs at the University of Idaho had provided 927 low-income students with assistance to complete school and obtain additional preparation for employment. Every graduating high school senior who participated was required to complete the Free Application for Federal Student Aid (FAFSA) as well as an application for admission to a college or university. Isabel's students would gather for recalls at her home or on campus and were required to fill out the FAFSA forms on the spot.

Although many did not pursue higher education, the seed of possibility had been planted for future generations. "Isabel exhibited her own ways of being to others and in this way showed by example," said forty-two-year-old Sydel Samuels, who began working with Isabel about a year after Isabel wrote the first Northwest Nations Upward Bound grant in 2000 to target Native American students from other tribes in the region in addition to the Nez Perce and Coeur d'Alene. "She had a great work ethic. She also believed in doing well by others and always giving back."[24]

Sydel is a Nez Perce from Lapwai with family on the Umatilla Reservation. "All the tribes in our area are part of one big community," she said. "And a lot of tribal members knew Isabel because of her long-standing work with the Nez Perce and Coeur d'Alene Tribes in particular."[25] Sydel first arrived on the U of I campus during high school as part of the Native American Internship Program that Isabel had established. The program was designed to allow some students to work alongside Upward Bound participants. "She found jobs on campus during summers for four to five students," added Sydel, who earned a bachelor's degree and a master's degree in public administration.[26]

Sydel worked for her tribe in social services before returning to campus in 2013. Today, she is director of the Native American Student Center at U of I. Back in 2001, she went to work for Tona TreeTop, who was supervised by Isabel at the Northwest Nations Upward Bound program. In 2002, Sydel applied for the Northwest Nations Upward Bound coordinator position and held that job until 2004. During that period, Isabel served as director of the TRIO programs at U of I, which included Upward Bound, Upward Bound Math and Science, Northwest Nations Upward Bound, Talent Search, and the HOIST program. "Isabel was a tireless worker who would show up earlier than anyone in the morning and not leave until late at night. Even after work she would go meet with someone who needed her help or go to cultural or other community events. I don't think I ever saw her go home," said Sydel.[27]

The Northwest Nations Upward Bound program was created by Isabel to serve ten Northwest tribes. "She was very knowledgeable about individual people and about university programs. She collected research materials and newspaper articles all year long to support her grant-writing projects." Sydel said she thinks the reach of Upward Bound may have decreased since Isabel left the program in 2006. "I think once Isabel left, the personal knowledge about all these tribes decreased and the connections were greatly reduced," she noted.[28]

Sydel's father, Bryan Samuels, a former principal at Lapwai High School, had been retired for some time, but he came out of retirement to work under Chris Meyer at the Coeur d'Alene Tribe's Education Department. "Isabel was the person who first brought my father to the University of Idaho," said Sydel. "She was a tireless advocate who would push you to meet or exceed your capabilities and support you for as long as she possibly could. She definitely created a generational shift toward education attainment for my family."[29]

DEFYING THE ODDS

By 2000, Isabel had received numerous awards, including the President's Medallion for outstanding service to the University of Idaho. She also succeeded in writing a successful grant for the College Assistance Migrant Program (CAMP) at the University of Idaho. CAMP served migrant workers, including Upward Bound student Jessica Samuels, a woman of African American descent who grew up in the reservation town of Orofino, Idaho, and is not related to Sydel Samuels.

Raised by her Hungarian-Norwegian mother and Nez Perce stepfather, Jessica, now forty-two, defies easy categorization regarding ethnicity. The oldest of four siblings and a victim of sexual abuse from the age of five, Jessica had the odds stacked against her finishing high school, much less attending college. Her parents passed away when she was a young woman, leaving her responsible for the care of her younger siblings.[30]

Jessica achieved high test scores in seventh grade and lettered at sports. Sadly, the disintegration of her family due to drug use and other issues led to her moving from one town to another. Jessica met Isabel when she was thirteen, after Jessica's mother had taken her five children to stay in a hotel in Clarkston, Washington, so that she could collect a bigger welfare check than was offered in Idaho. "Luckily, I had a social worker who knew about my troubles at home," said Jessica. "Upward Bound changed everything. It opened a whole new world for me. Where I came from in Orofino, I was at best a mediocre student, but the Upward Bound teachers really cared about us. They were young and gung ho and really wanted to reach out to their students."[31]

Despite having missed many days of school, Jessica scored high enough on an Upward Bound placement test to be in a science class designed for seniors. "John Crout taught life skills class and weight training," said Jessica. "He was the first black person, other than myself, who I had ever met, and I was thirteen years old. Isabel introduced me to him and we became very good friends. Even the Indians didn't seem to like blacks very much. Racism is something that is taught and perhaps exists mostly in people's imaginations, but it is real. People give it enough validity that it becomes real."[32]

Jessica thrived in the Upward Bound program, returning later to live in the dorms during summers to oversee younger students. "Upward Bound gave me a lot of confidence and the structure I did not have at home. It allowed me to feel safe. It also took me away from that whole family environment of chaos and drugs and alcohol to someplace I could focus on me and on being a student. Most importantly, Upward Bound opened my eyes to the possibility of going to college. This was no longer an abstract idea."[33]

Jessica was able to graduate from high school, get a cosmetology license, and then earn a bachelor's degree in sociology with a minor in Native American studies. She worked for Upward Bound on a number of occasions as a dormitory counselor, eventually earning an academic certificate in diversity and stratification and a master's degree in public administration.

CAMP proved essential for Jessica, who had worked for the US Forest Service, driving migrant tree planters to their jobs. The program assists students who are migratory or seasonal farm workers (or children of such workers) enrolled in their first year of undergraduate studies. Isabel had seen that the federal government was going to expand funding for CAMP nationwide and wrote a grant for U of I. She realized that Jessica qualified for the program and enrolled her in it.

Jessica Samuels attended law school classes for a period of time. She divorced her husband while she was in law school, only to find out during spring break that she was pregnant with her fourth child. "I realized that I could not do law school, but I decided instead to go for my master's degree. I had my fourth child on Thursday and was back in class by Monday. I am dedicated, but only because I have had people like Isabel that are dedicated to me. There has been too much time and too many people's focus put into me to just let it go. I also want to be an example for my children."[34]

While she was still in high school, Jessica joined Isabel on a trip to Boise State University for a weekend "Black to the Future" conference organized when BSU was trying to recruit African American students to Idaho. "We drove down and were shown around campus. I was only a junior in high school and was excited to know that there would be other black people there, but I did not know what to expect."[35]

Rosa Parks, a hero of the American Civil Rights movement, was introduced at the conference and gave a short talk about her experience.

Jessica recalled, "I had learned that Rosa Parks refused to get up from her seat on the bus and in this way started the boycott that ended segregation. But meeting her was not as important at the time as it was later. Many of us went up on stage and had our picture taken with her, but sometimes things like this don't impact you until much later in life."[36]

Today, Jessica puts her personal experience to work as an academic success counselor at the University of Idaho, helping a new generation of students overcome challenges. Yet challenges persist. "Last fall when I graduated with a master's degree, I did not find a job right away. It takes a long time to find a position in academia. Last summer I was homeless with four children. Isabel opened her door and had us stay with her for six weeks. We had nowhere else to go," said Jessica, adding, "I can only hope to one day help as many people as Isabel has."[37]

In 2001, Isabel received the Martin Luther King Jr. Distinguished Service Award on behalf of the University of Idaho and Washington State University. Ten years after she and Jessica traveled to meet Rosa Parks in Boise, Isabel was awarded the 2003 Rosa Parks Award for Contributions to Diversity at the University of Idaho.

Times have changed since the earliest days of Upward Bound, and Upward Bound has changed with the times. When the program began, it served mostly Native Americans, but today it is much more diverse, as are Moscow and Idaho in general. "The program continues to serve first-generation college candidates. But today they are not only native but Anglo, Hispanic, Asian, and from Eastern European countries," said Jessica.[38]

Chapter 13

NEW GENERATION

MONA DANIELS, age thirty-five, is among the second generation of students who participated in Upward Bound at U of I during Isabel Bond's tenure as director of the program. Mona was raised in Plummer and spent most of her childhood in the foster care system. Today she lives in Worley and works as a senior case specialist for the Coeur d'Alene Tribe's Child Support Program, which she helped develop. "I enjoy my job. I like what I do, and it is cool to be working for my tribe," said Mona, who is Nez Perce. "I am thankful for Upward Bound and will always be grateful for everything Isabel did for me in high school."[1]

In 1999, Mona joined a group of students from Mullan to attend Upward Bound in Moscow. She had two older sisters and three older brothers, several of whom also attended Upward Bound. "I thought it was some kind of summer camp," said Mona. She discovered in high school that the program could be used for academic credit retrieval. "I was really struggling during my sophomore and junior years with math credits. Upward Bound helped me in my problem areas. Throughout the school year, the Upward Bound coordinator at our high school was in touch with Isabel's program. They stayed in touch with us to make sure we were on track and gave us incentives to get ready for college."[2]

Mona enjoyed the atmosphere at Upward Bound and the taste of college life it offered. "Being on the U of I campus was very different than being on the rez. I made a lot of friends. After the summer, we took trips together to the University of Idaho Vandals football game and the Washington State University Cougars games."[3]

Mona had always been interested in education and wanted to go to college, but she faced challenges while growing up in the foster care system. "My mother and father separated shortly after I was born. I went to live with my mother, but she was heavily involved in drugs and alcohol. She was too far off into her addictions and was not able to pull out of it," said Mona, who was placed in various foster homes. "In one of my first family placements, I was physically abused and said nothing for a long time. I finally told my father, and he went to court to get me back. I did not live with him until I was ten years old."[4]

Mona applied herself to her studies, determined to someday help kids who had gone through circumstances similar to her own. Her Upward Bound high school coordinator, Carol Harsh, offered study skills and tutoring. "She gave five of us rides from the Coeur d'Alene Reservation to Spokane Community College, which was the only place you could take an ACT [American College Testing] test. I wanted to gain a new experience and go to Seattle. Isabel encouraged me to go after what I wanted."[5]

Mona was initially denied admission to the University of Washington because she was from out of state, but Isabel got in touch with Native American recruiters in Seattle who understood the appeals process. "She got the information and passed it on to me, and I wrote a statement about why I should be admitted, with more personal history about the adversity I faced growing up, my life experience, and what I planned to do with my future. I also collected some letters of recommendation from teachers."[6]

Mona earned a bachelor's degree in social welfare with a minor in American Indian studies. She then earned a master's degree in social work from Eastern Washington University. "Social work is a broad field," she said. "I have a lot of empathy for kids who go through the same situations I went through." Mona worked for a while for Indian Child

Welfare, which is similar to Child Protective Services. On the reservation, this is a difficult job. "It is hard to separate your work from your personal life and not bring it home with you," she said.[7]

In 2009, a position opened up on the tribe's Child Support Program. Mona applied for the job and transferred to Worley to accept the position, helping to adapt the program for local needs. The math skills she learned at Upward Bound still come in handy; today, she supervises two other caseworkers and makes calculations for monthly child support obligations for noncustodial parents. "The Child Support Program has been around in the state system for some time, but it is fairly new to our tribe," said Mona. "I truly loved and valued my experience at the University of Washington, but I always wanted to give back to my people and work for my tribe and make an impact somehow."[8] Today she does.

SOLDIERING ON

David Taptto, age forty-four, is the son of a Kiowa father and Nez Perce mother. He was born in Oklahoma, raised in Lapwai, and served in the US Marines from 1996 until 2006. He was severely injured, nearly losing a leg to amputation, and is today completing college studies that will allow him to help other veterans survive the traumas of war. "Isabel was always in the back of my mind when I was going through the darkest times because I always heard her nagging, concerned, worried, and ultimately motivational voice through it all," said David.[9]

In 1989, David joined the summer Upward Bound program to do something different: "I had friends in the program, and I wanted to get away from the reservation, to do something other than hang around Lapwai all summer." David had never been to a college campus before. He moved into Targhee Hall with reservations friends, including guys he names only as "Yummers, Dennis, and Brad." The U of I campus was a far cry from the town of Lapwai: "I thought, 'So this is what a campus of higher education looks like.' All I knew about university life was what I had seen on television and what our teachers had told us. I have to say that when I went there, I was in awe of the place."

The Native American residence hall advisors and staff members that Isabel hired at Upward Bound made David feel less out of place. "The instructors were top-notch. They made the transition as easy as possible for us because they knew many of us had never been to a campus before. The students all clicked as a group," he said.[10]

Upward Bound focused him on his studies but also provided recreational opportunities he would not have had back on the reservation: "We went bowling at the Student Union Building. One weekend, we went rafting and camping on the Selway River. Another weekend, we went on a trip to the Columbia River and camped at spots throughout the entire road trip. All of these were full of great memories and good times. Yet Isabel held the line when it came to showing up for classes."

"I think Isabel knew how rambunctious reservation kids could be, so she ruled with an iron fist. She was strict, but she was also fair," said David, adding "I'd have to say that the first summer I was there I did not care for her very much." He received a minor infraction for being three minutes late for the ten o'clock curfew. "I was just down the road at the girls dorm, and I thought I had one minute left. But Isabel gave zero leeway. In the big picture years later, I can see that this is understandable, but at the time I thought, 'Ten minutes? Seriously, Isabel?'"[11]

By the following year, David's grades were sufficient to move ahead until his use of alcohol progressed and he found himself in need of rehabilitation during the middle of the school year. "My junior year was pretty rough. I missed an entire quarter because I was away at a treatment center in Vancouver, Washington. The following summer I needed Upward Bound in order to stay current with my graduating class, and I really needed it just to graduate," he said.[12]

Fresh out of rehab, David needed encouragement to get through the summer and on to his senior year. "I don't know if Isabel knew my situation and how much I needed her program at the time. She may not have known, but I felt her constant push in everything that summer. I found out that Isabel really cares about us. She pushed me to succeed, and she has been pushing me ever since," he noted.[13]

Persistence paid off for the U of I Upward Bounders that summer when they competed in the Knowledge Bowl against other Upward Bound programs from across the Northwest, including Portland and Seattle. David, his cousin Catherine, and two others were part of the Knowledge Bowl competition. "It was really fun. Our Moscow Upward Bound program won third place. Isabel and my cousin Catherine were great supporters of me. It seemed like every conversation that year with Isabel always led me to positive and motivating feelings."[14]

Thanks to Isabel's encouragement and the hard work of the entire Upward Bound staff, David was able to persevere. He graduated with his class and the following year attended a college preparatory summer session at the University of Colorado, sponsored by the Council of Energy Resource Tribes (CERT). There, he met Jennifer Alcott, a Navajo woman who later became his wife and the mother of their three daughters, Gwendolyn, Adrianna Jo, and Kristen. "She always was an extremely beautiful and intelligent lady. Her intelligence has always exceeded mine from that summer we met up to now. She is the only woman in the entire universe that has been verifiably known to be smarter than one David Taptto," he said with a chuckle. "She still has my heart."[15]

David returned to Nez Perce country to attend Lewis-Clark State College, situated in Lewiston about twelve miles from Lapwai. During the summer of 1993, he worked at Upward Bound as a resident advisor. While attending LCSC, he got back into some bad habits. "I didn't do so well, partly because I was back home and hanging out with my crazy friends who were 'taking time off,' and so I was not focused on my studies," David said. After the fall 1993 semester, he traveled to Arizona to visit his girlfriend:

> It was kind of a culture shock for me down there in Navajo country. People sometimes think all native cultures are the same, but they are very different. An entire book can be written on the different beliefs between our two cultures. If one does not have a clear understanding of the various cultural diversities from the start, then it becomes

> almost impossible to explain how a belief in one culture can have a huge impact on another's spiritual and physical well-being. For example, snakes are extremely evil and do render the need for ceremonial doings for Navajos. The Nimiipuu do not go through any of that for snakes. This is just one example.
>
> The Nimiipuu have our own beliefs, and the Navajo have theirs. I had to learn a lot of Navajo customs, as did Jennifer, for all of us to be healthy spiritually and physically. Navajos don't have sweat lodges like we do, but almost every home instead has a hogan, which is significant in so many ways and can mean so many things. It can be the centerpiece of the family. Some hogans are kept strictly for ceremonial uses. Some families live in them. Up here, we are working extremely hard to maintain our language. The Navajos are fluent in their language, and my daughters all understand Navajo and speak it fluently. It's all they speak to one another. English is the fallback, universal language when one does not speak Navajo.[16]

Soon David and Jennifer were expecting Gwen, the first of their three daughters. "I was trying to find any job I could to bring in money to raise our daughter," said David. "I told Jennifer I was thinking about joining the military. She didn't like the idea at first, but the truth is, I joined up to support my family."[17]

In September 1996, David joined the United States Marine Corps. His home duty station was at Camp Pendleton in San Diego. His first deployment out of country was in 1999 to Okinawa, Japan, for one year, unaccompanied by his wife and daughter. During that year, Jennifer and Gwen moved back to Arizona.

After coming back from Okinawa, David was reassigned to the Third Battalion, First Marine Regiment, which is part of the First Marine Division. In 2001, the infantry unit deployed on a navy ship to sail around the western Pacific as a force in readiness. The ship was attacked by terrorists on the tiny Kuwaiti island of Faylaka. "Two Marines of Lima Company were gunned down, and that day turned into a twelve-hour war. It was the first contact any of us experienced with another human being who was trying to end our lives."[18]

Later that summer, the Taptto family was together at Camp Pendleton, where David began training for another western Pacific deployment. On September 11, 2001, Jennifer dropped David off very early because his unit was heading to the field for a week or two and had to draw weapons from the armory at four in the morning:

> In the middle of our work-up trainings, the 9/11 terrorist attacks took place in New York City and the Pentagon. We held formation at five in the morning and were told to go find the closest television and watch these events unfold. We were given instructions to muster back on the parade deck at eight o'clock. It became evident to me that we would soon be going to war. This became our motivation as we trained. My thoughts were with Jennifer and our daughters throughout training. I joined the military for our family, and I was going to do my part to protect my family and our country.[19]

David was with one of the first units deployed during the 2003 Iraq invasion. He rode with a military convoy from the Kuwait border to Baghdad. His last tour in Iraq took place in November 2004 with the Third Battalion, First Marine Division, Lima Company in the embattled Iraq city of Fallujah. Insurgents were overrunning David's unit as they took over the city. The decision was passed down to send in the infantry and retake it from the insurgents. The Marines' Third Battalion, First Division was among other Marine infantry divisions and army units to undertake Operation Phantom Fury:

> I recall the early morning hours, surrounding the city before we went in, watching the army unload round after round of tank fire and everything else you can imagine. It was like the Fourth of July. We were just dug in at that point, in fighting holes watching it, bullshitting, catnapping, talking about home, waiting. In the early morning hours, a small platoon from the Iraqi Army was tasked with attacking

> the train station outside of Fallujah to gain a foothold for us to begin our assault on the city.[20]

Soon David's unit was many city blocks into the city, engaged in house-to-house urban warfare. "All the battalions were on the line. My squad was in an alley with our four amtraks [amphibious assault vehicles]. We were the reserve element on an assault that was taking place by my platoon at that time. The enemy had a spotter in one of the buildings and unleashed precise mortar fire on us, followed by small arms fire, medium machine gun fire, rocket-propelled grenades. You name it, we got it." An explosion destroyed most of David's lower left leg, sent shrapnel through his neck, and lodged a piece of metal in his heart. "My flak jacket and neck protector saved my life, and so did my squad medic. Somebody performed an emergency tracheotomy on me, and I was med-evacuated to an aid station. I remember one of the priests reading me my last rites and granting me absolution while I was on the table."[21]

A Thousand Miles to Baghdad, a book by Darrin Mortenson and Hayne Palmour IV, is about the invasion David took part in, which began more than a decade of conflict in the region. David's injuries were severe. He deliberated with surgeons for two weeks over whether to endure a long, painful recovery or have his lower left leg amputated. He decided to keep it, but David's journey back to his family at Camp Pendleton and eventually to his community at Lapwai marked the beginning of an intensification of addiction issues that had begun long before.

"I had always loved to drink," he said. "So, I had this period of darkness where I was basically drunk from 2005 until 2012. I was drinking heavily even while I was in the hospitals. I got off-ward privileges and wanted to be away from the daily visual reminder of the ongoing war. I escaped to the bars, any bar, and I would be back in time to take my medications and leave again. I forgot about everything and everyone that had supported me. Even my daughters fell by the wayside. I tried to commit suicide a few times while I was going through this darkness. In the end, I lost the love of my life to divorce." During this dark period, David said, he ran into Isabel Bond a few times. By then, she was working with Phil Allen in Lapwai at the Northwest Indian College. "She would always ask me, 'Well, David, what are you doing now? You need to get back into college. You need to come see me.' She would say, 'We can do this.'"[22]

It took a third felony driving under the influence (DUI) offense to bring David around to the realization that he had to change his ways. He went into the rehabilitation program at the VA medical center in Walla Walla, Washington, for thirty days of treatment, after which they immediately sent him to the Puget Sound VA facility at American Lake, for intensive inpatient post-traumatic stress disorder (PTSD) treatment for another thirty days.

"In the twelve-step program, they talk about a spiritual awakening. For me it was more like the creator's hand came down and said, 'Enough is enough.' Lo and behold, they were starting a veterans' treatment court in Lewiston during this period of my journey." Rather than face jail time, David joined the innovative Veterans Treatment Court in 2013. The judge required him to undergo treatment for PTSD, go to weekly psychological counseling sessions, and attend AA meetings with other veterans.

> I had to face the things that I had avoided reliving. I had to face the memories of what I experienced over there where I lost good friends. I had struggled for so long with myself, saying I should have done this or that differently, but the fact is that we are human and are not perfect, especially under an enormous amount of stress. That's a tough pill to swallow when it involves another bro's life, because that is the point where I expect to be 200 percent perfect all of the time.[23]

David said the Veterans Treatment Court afforded him the opportunity to go back to college, where he has studied new perspectives on military trauma, preparing him to one day help others. "Going through therapy has opened my eyes. I had been looking at myself as weak for not dealing with things in a manlier way, but now I have learned how PTSD feeds alcoholism, and how alcoholism in turn feeds

PTSD. They are closely intertwined and are blood relatives when you think about it."[24]

David is in his junior year of studies toward a degree in social work, with minors in addiction studies and psychology. He has written term papers on the physiological effects of combat trauma and the exhausting experience of reliving memories from war. He hopes to pass on what he has learned to other returning veterans.

> I love to help people. Social work is a versatile degree, but I am a veteran. We are a country that will always be at war, and each generation of veterans has its own challenges. It has been a long journey back for me. I want to help other veterans come back home also. Isabel always knew how to get around a roadblock. I eventually helped myself get back into college, but she was the primary reason; the big influence to try it one last time. I still think of her when I get good grades.[25]

Chapter 14

CHIEF LOOKING GLASS POWWOW

UPWARD BOUND succeeded by showing Native American students that the pursuit of a higher education can go hand in hand with the exploration and preservation of their culture. The accultura-tion between individuals from diverse backgrounds in the program has contributed to a new era of tolerance and mutual understanding that is unfolding in northern Idaho today.

Even so, the Nez Perce War of 1877 remains emblematic of the many conflicts between Native Americans and European Americans that will forever mark the history of North America. In Indian Country, one way to move forward is to recall the past in ceremony and song. To remember is to heal.

About an hour's drive upstream from Lapwai through the nar-row canyon of the Clearwater River is the town of Kamiah and the home of the upriver Nez Perce. On a sunny August day in 2014, food trucks and craft stands slowly assembled in town behind the Wa-A'Yas Community Center for the weekend's Chief Looking Glass Powwow. Bleachers were set in a circle around an arena within the wide lawn that surrounds the building. Tents and tepees went up behind the bleachers. The central arena was festooned with strands of light bulbs reaching out from a central pole, and a plywood announcer's stand stood above the arena.

The town was built in the heart of traditional Nez Perce territory on a gently sloping, open area at the confluence of the Clearwater River and Lawyer Creek. The town was segregated one hundred years ago, with Native Americans living and worshipping in neighborhoods separate from whites, who still own most of the downtown commercial district.

The hills that surround Kamiah are dotted with vacation homes. There are numerous shops, bars, and restaurants on Main Street that cater to tourists, including many who visit the nearby Nez Perce National Historical Park sites. There are also grocery stores, a small casino, restaurants, souvenir shops, and a historical museum that celebrates Native American culture as well as Lewis and Clark's Corps of Discovery expedition. The Kamiah Welcome Center sports a small museum that displays numerous artifacts from the trapping era. A series of four large paintings depict idealized Nez Perce camps as they would have looked during each of the four seasons, prior to European contact. Indian culture and history are part and parcel of the tourism industry here.

BRINGING PEOPLE TOGETHER

About a block off the bottom of Main Street is the small It'se Ye-Ye Casino, where locals and tourists hunch, smoking, over slot machines late into the night. Next door is Kamiah's Nimiipuu Health Clinic. Adjacent to both buildings are the gymnasium, kitchens, and meeting rooms that make up the Nez Perce Wa-A'Yas Community Center. This bustling building serves as an all-purpose meeting hall and sports complex. It also houses the Nez Perce Tribe's Head Start program.

During a four-on-four basketball tournament early in the day before the evening powwow, young men and women competed while others looked on and cheered. One of the players, a teenage white boy with strawberry blond hair in tightly plaited braids addressed a nearby elderly Nez Perce woman as "Grandmother." Zachary Broncheau, a lieutenant with the Kamiah Police Department, dominated the court, taking reliable drop shots on the basket from outside the ring.

The Nez Perce Wheeler family organizes the Chief Looking Glass Powwow annually to celebrate the legacy of their ancestor, Looking Glass, son of Ippakness Wayhayken (Looking Glass around Neck), who was drawn reluctantly into the war of 1877 and killed at the Battle of Bear Paw near Havre, Montana.

In preparation for the powwow's opening ceremony, a large group of Native American people from many tribes, dressed in full regalia, gathered at the top of Main Street. A Nez Perce woman stood up across from the Welcome Center and sang the American national anthem over a loudspeaker. After a round of applause from hundreds of spectators, a procession of powwow dancers, veterans, schoolchildren, and their families and friends drove, walked, and rode down Main Street—past the slyly named Looking Glass Eye Center, past the gravestone maker, and the bars, cafes, and stores—to the Wa-A'Yas Community Center.

Several members of the Wheeler family are former Upward Bound students. They had attended to various details for the event, helping to set up the arbors and powwow arena outside. Horace Axtell, age ninety, was helped from his automobile to a seat inside the community center auditorium, where dozens of tables and hundreds of chairs had been set up in preparation for a salmon feast that was to feed about three hundred people.

Isabel arrived early and searched out and greeted people to discuss personal matters with some of her former students and their relatives. Relatives returning from outside the community greeted elders. Ceremonial words were shared about the salmon and its significance to the tribe. Many Native American families and non-Indian friends and relatives were served buffet-style by young people.

When everyone was finished, the tables and chairs were cleared to make room for a large group of visitors from various tribes who were there to perform the Gourd Dance, an honoring ceremony for "war mothers"—women who have lost brothers, sons, and fathers in military conflicts. A drumming and singing group took position and began to sing in the distinctive style of western tribes. Behind them stood a row of Native American men who had traveled to Nez Perce country to perform the dance, which originated in Kiowa country many generations ago. Women of all ages, including grandmothers, mothers, and granddaughters, lined up at one side of the auditorium, each separated by a man from the community who stood at her side for support. Most of the men were military veterans.

One by one, these women told their stories—about a brother lost in Iraq, a father lost in Vietnam, a distant relative who fell during the 1877 Nez Perce War. Not one of the women was left to bear her burden alone. People in the audience had tears in their eyes as the women opened up and mourned freely. Each of the women was held in ceremony by the entire community in this group ritual of mourning and healing.

The men then took turns describing their military experiences. A Special Forces veteran named the company he served with in Vietnam in 1968. Two aging World War II veterans recalled the units they fought in during the war in Europe. A younger vet, wearing desert fatigues from Afghanistan or Iraq, told of his duty overseas; he then mentioned a distant grandfather who fell during the 1877 war. These men were honored publicly for their service in protecting their families, their communities, and their country.

HONORING TRADITION, CELEBRATING THE FUTURE

The men performing the Gourd Dance wore ribbon shirts in the style of many East Coast and Midwest tribes. They were Ojibwa or Sioux, and there were also men from West Coast tribes, one of whom was a college professor in Seattle. One of the dancers described how the dance began many generations ago in Kiowa country, how the rattles they used were said to mimic the sound of arrows in the quivers of warriors as they ran through the forest, a comforting sound to families who might otherwise have been left vulnerable to attack. An Ojibwa man and war veteran explained to the community that thirty-five Indian nations today practice the Gourd Dance. He told of how this Kiowa tradition began with a song originally given to them by Red Wolf—a character of myth and legend—and how the tradition had now been passed down through many generations. He said that performing the dance of Red Wolf in Nez Perce country resonated with the Nez Perce Tribe's role in helping reintroduce wolves to Idaho.

The drumming and singing of the dancers filled the auditorium, leading to high, piercing notes, as the women stood solemnly and listened, or swayed together, grieving for their losses and for one another. People gathered long afterward to console one another and talk before walking outside to the powwow. At dusk, the area behind Wa-A'Yas was illuminated by the strings of light bulbs that reached outward to the perimeter of the circular powwow arena. Groups of men sat around large drums, laughing and talking. At one drum, a young man from the West Coast wore a white T-shirt that said, "Got Land? Thank an Indian."

People milled about and settled onto the grass and into the bleachers with fry bread and Indian tacos. At the center of the arena, an announcer welcomed several individuals, including some veterans, and then a woman from the tribe welcomed a group of police officers, including Zachary Broncheau, the Nez Perce basketball player, now wearing a crisp blue and black police uniform and a tight braid. The announcer, a woman from Kamiah, thanked the officers for fighting the good fight against the single most threatening enemy of the Nez Perce Tribe—methamphetamine, a drug that has ravaged the community in recent years.

Soon the powwow announcer started cracking jokes and bringing the dancers out in groups, tiny tots first, then traditional, then fancy dancers. Phil Allen, dressed in spectacular fancy-dance regalia, took a break from drumming and smiled at his daughter as she sprang back and forth among the many tiny-tot competitors who spun and bounced in bright-colored regalia under the lights. In Kamiah, near the Heart of the Monster and close to where the Nez Perce first encountered European Americans more than two hundred years ago, Native American people were celebrating a bright future.

Epilogue

◈ THE CHANGING OF THE GUARD ◈

ISABEL WAS seventy-three years old in 2006 when she was dismissed from her position as director of Upward Bound following reported behavior and discipline problems on campus with some of the program's participants. At the time, university officials declined to provide details, citing confidentiality rules concerning personnel matters, but they indicated that Isabel's termination was related in part to policy changes.[1] Michael Highfill served as interim coordinator of Upward Bound while Isabel was on administrative leave in 2005. He said at the time that demand for the program had grown and that stricter federal guidelines were being implemented that required minimum grade point averages for students to qualify for the program.[2]

Isabel claimed publicly that U of I intended to reduce support for at-risk students who needed the program most. She appealed her dismissal to the Idaho State Board of Education, which deadlocked over whether to hear her case, and so the appeal failed. Eventually, her office was cleared out and she left campus.

Camille (Arthur) Wynecoop signed a petition demanding Isabel's reinstatement. She told a news reporter in 2005 that the program was suffering in Isabel's absence. "I know a lot of people who have signed the petition and who are appalled that Isabel has not regained her position as the head of Upward Bound," she said, adding, "Her position is very significant in Indian country."[3] Wynecoop was one of many Native American students who benefited from Isabel's dedication and personal attention. She attended Upward Bound for three years and lived on and off at Isabel's house while working toward a college degree. She eventually earned a master's in education and now works as a college and career specialist for the Coeur d'Alene Tribe.[4]

Since Isabel's departure, the Upward Bound program that she developed and expanded has evolved in many ways. In part, this can be attributed to policy maintenance at the federal level and amendments to the Higher Education Act of 1965, which originally authorized the TRIO programs, noted Scott Clyde, who currently oversees the Upward Bound program.[5]

These changes, coupled with society's changing expectations of public institutions of higher education, have caused the university's management of the TRIO programs to become increasingly informed by grant compliance, risk mitigation, and measurable participant outcomes. For students in the original target areas, this has resulted in splitting Upward Bound into three separate programs: one for Silver Valley, a second for Lapwai and Orofino, and a third for Kamiah and Clearwater Valley.[6]

Northwest Nations Upward Bound was scaled back from serving ten tribes in three states to three tribes in one state, and now serves only the Coeur d'Alene Tribe. This reduction in target area has allowed for one full-time Upward Bound outreach coordinator to be assigned to each of the target schools in the remaining service area. The Upward Bound Math and Science Project, which Isabel initiated, has similarly evolved as a result of policy maintenance at the federal level. Originally conceived as a regional center that primarily provided summer programming to students nominated for participation from around the Northwest, including Alaska, today it also provides in-school services during the academic year for STEM-focused students attending target high schools in the Lewis Clark Valley.[7]

Scott Clyde—a nephew of Isabel's—supervises a suite of outreach and engagement projects at the University of Idaho, including the original

Upward Bound program. He has witnessed the program's evolution and can attest to Isabel's influence.

> While the Upward Bound project at the University of Idaho has evolved in response to a number of influences—shifting federal priorities, evolving societal norms, budgetary considerations, as well as technological and pedagogical innovations—Isabel's legacy of commitment to native scholars, the rich insights that they bring to education at all levels and the valuable contributions that they make to a diverse society, continues to influence the University of Idaho to this day. Individuals she mentored have positions of influence on campus; programs she initiated continue to serve natives and non-natives alike both on and off tribal reservations; and initiatives she envisioned to serve native scholars at the institution have been adopted and implemented.
>
> From my perspective, what Isabel demonstrated over the course of her tenure has become integral to the university's identity as a land grant institution—a commitment to educational access for historically underrepresented learners, including and especially those who have lived since time immemorial on the land from which the land grant was made. I believe it is in this regard that the spirit of Isabel lives on.[8]

In October 2014, only a few months after work on this book began, Isabel took a fall and has been slowly recovering in an eldercare facility in Moscow. By the time of her injury, Isabel had made it clear that any book about her work for Upward Bound should be less about her and more about her students and their careers.

Only a small number of the two-thousand-plus students served by Isabel and her teachers at Upward Bound gave interviews for this book, but their stories span over four decades and reflect the sometimes profound impact Upward Bound and Isabel Bond had on their lives. Several of them provided updates on activities since their student days.

Chris Meyer continues to oversee the Coeur d'Alene Tribe's Department of Education. She said her tribe is using education to take responsibility for essential tasks related to self-governance, attending to natural resource preservation, managing forests, and working to become good stewards for the children. Yet she remains concerned about high Native American dropout rates at the Plummer-Worley high school. She said almost all of the nineteen tribal government directors are Coeur d'Alenes, but the next tier down is mostly non-native. These include early childhood schoolteachers, program managers, and natural resource workers. "When we get native Coeur d'Alene people leading these programs, we will have a different mindset. When you are born into a tribe, you have an expanded sense of responsibility, you are not only responsible to your immediate family but also to your wider tribal community."[9]

Otis Halfmoon recently retired after serving the National Park Service as an American Indian services specialist, working to increase the number of indigenous employees within the National Park system and retain those already employed. One of his major focus points was to include tribal stories at National Park Service sites. In the course of his work, he consulted with over 150 federally recognized tribes.

Otis has come far from that first lesson offered by an Upward Bound instructor with a set of bagpipes. He worked with a wide diversity of Native American people around the United States. His wife, Virginia, is a member of the Pueblo of Santa Clara in New Mexico. She has exposed him to the many dances, ceremonies, and traditions of her people. "I have seen how these Pueblo tribes have incorporated the Catholic traditions side by side with the traditional ceremonies. I think the Nez Perce could learn from them to repair the schism between Christians and traditionals," he said.[10]

Thirty-three years after attending Upward Bound, Bob Wheaton is a high school teacher in California. He is currently collaborating on a National Science Foundation grant to develop a Native American-based mathematics curriculum for integration into undergraduate courses. This is being done in partnership with California State University at Fullerton and Turtle Mountain Community College in Belcourt, North Dakota. "It has been fun using my history and science, adding cultural relevancy to mathematics. Native Americans did use mathematical ideas, but they were not written down. They used them in stories. We often give no credit to their awareness of the world around them," said Bob.[11]

He sees his own trajectory, first as a student and then as a teacher, in a wider perspective. "I grew up in a tribal culture where elders spoke first and were respected, not those who are most aggressive. A lot of white people in power don't think but speak first. A lot of clashes in my career have come from this. On the rez, you give a lot of respect to elders, who are assimilating information before they speak. I really don't fit into the mainstream culture. It is a different world."[12]

Bob has worked on research that shows the dangers of using blood quantum percentages as the sole means for tribal status, which he said has become the norm only after some tribes became flush with new financial resources from gaming revenue. "Tribal enrollment used to be about community recognition also," he said. "Tribes have the authority to designate whatever criteria they want for inclusion, but they limit themselves to criteria devised for them by the BIA instead of using traditional ideas. Tribes should get together and realize that the success of the tribe depends ultimately on their per capita numbers. Otherwise, we can go extinct."[13]

Bob said contemporary concerns such as these are often what subsequent generations of educated Native American students evolve toward. He said the first concern is basic survival, but new perspectives can sometimes lead to new career opportunities. "The first generation of people to become educated often become teachers because that is whom they can identify with. But we eventually become more introspective about our place in the world. The next generations might become exposed to doctors and lawyers and other professions," he said.[14]

Bob teaches his students that history is not always about society's so-called "winners"—it is also about those members of society who have contributed in more diverse ways. The Southern California school system where he teaches is predominantly Hispanic, yet this population is underrepresented in what he describes as a "top down" hierarchy. "I end up defending these kids in many ways," he said. "The Mexican governmental education system has been so successful at assimilation that many of my Hispanic students do not realize they are Native Americans. I say, 'Look at your skin. You are native, not European.'"[15]

Bill Picard, as vice chairman of the Nez Perce Tribe, continues to stand up for tribal sovereignty and treaty rights, which are inextricably linked to the continued understanding of the tribe's history. He is quick to point out that the Battle of Bear Paw in 1877 ended a war but did not mark the end of Nez Perce history. Some Nez Perce did reach the Lakota Sioux camp of Chief Sitting Bull. "The history books say it ended when Joseph surrendered," said Picard, "but Chief White Bird and two hundred Nez Perce made it into Canada, along with Chief Joseph's daughter. Many of them are now part of the Blood (Kainai) and Piegan Blackfeet Tribes. First Nations in Canada have much better relations with their government than US tribes do."[16]

Picard took the study skills and personal encouragement he received at Upward Bound and turned them into success in college and a long career of service as an educator and tribal leader. Over the years, he has focused considerable time and energy on the preservation and development of tribal fisheries, sometimes in opposition to the plans of utility companies whose dams have devastated runs of steelhead and Chinook salmon, a traditional food source of the Nez Perce and neighboring tribes. "We have retained our culture, but the biggest impact to our fisheries has been the fifteen dams between here and the ocean," said Picard. "They kill half the fish that go down over them, and on the way back up, the fish have to find fish ladders. At the lower dams right now, the fish are fed on by sea lions."[17]

The Nez Perce Tribe manages the largest Native American fish hatchery department in the United States, with two federal hatcheries and one state hatchery. Picard learned to fish in the old traditional way with his father and has passed on the tradition to his son. "We work government to government, with Idaho, Oregon, and Montana, and within aboriginal areas with the Umatilla, Warm Springs, and Yakama tribes, all of whom have fished traditionally on the Columbia River. We have been asking for better flows in dams, but the utility companies make their money off electricity, so they don't always think it is important enough to keep the flows strong for the fish. It's all in the name of recreation and electricity." Picard said that stagnant water stacked up behind each dam has caused oxygen depletion. Rising water temperatures have caused infections in fish gills. To make his point during a meeting with Bonneville Power Administration executives, he put a glass of water on the table and said to them: "If we left this water on the table for a week and came back, how many of you would drink it?"[18]

Lucinda George, Isabel Bond's early helper at Upward Bound, is now retired from a career in law enforcement and works part-time conducting interviews and doing research at the University of Idaho. After volunteering as a horse therapist for the Mounted Scholars program established by Isabel, George helped the tribe transition for the first time from Bureau of Indian Affairs police jurisdiction to a Nez Perce Tribal Police Department. "The BIA was not providing enough service for the 175-mile radius of the reservation, so I wrote a grant for eleven officers for the tribe and then recommended, at the request of our human resources director, Julian Matthews, a person to fill the role of chief of police. I recommended Tom Idle, from Puerto Rico. He and I had gone through the police academy together in Boise, and he had extensive background in the military."[19]

Through her association with Upward Bound and Isabel Bond, Lucinda was more readily able to promote the traditions of her tribe. "My husband at the time, Al Pinkham, came to the U of I during the Upward Bound sessions and told stories to the students. He provided a role model for them also," she said. Lucinda, Allen Pinkham, and many others attended a flag ceremony during the spring of 2017 at the United Methodist Church's Wallowa Lake Camp, in the center of the former homeland of Lucinda's band. "We raised a permanent Nez Perce flag for the first time over Wallowa Lake," she noted.[20]

Robert Seward, the student who came to Moscow from the mining town of Wallace, Idaho, now works in retail and stays in touch with some of his former Upward Bound classmates on Facebook. Others he has heard about through the grapevine. "One of my high school friends, Wayne Brenner, died in a mining accident. Another guy named Mark Flores got out of Upward Bound and did exactly what he said he was going to do—he got a two-year degree, and then joined the navy, and then joined the Special Forces. He had a plan, and he did it."[21]

Seward, now fifty-four, has found time for intellectual pursuits. He teaches an annual seminar at Lewis-Clark State College on the experience of German Americans and Japanese Americans during World War II. He is in the final stages of writing a historical novel based on the World War II internment camp at Crystal City, Texas, where German and Japanese Americans were kept under guard as prisoners. "I have read every book ever written on the subject and have talked to some of the survivors of the internment camps," he said.[22]

Chelle Merrill Josefowicz moved far away from Idaho and her Native American friends at Lapwai, yet she said her time among the Nez Perce shaped her life in many ways. Chelle and her husband live on the Tennessee River in Alabama, occasionally hunting buffalo carp fish with a traditional longbow equipped with a beaver skin grip. "They call it the Amazon of the south down here," said Chelle, who follows the Jewish faith of her husband. "You know, you can make really good latkes with buffalo carp."[23]

Each summer, Chelle and her husband join a group of thousands of motorcyclists who ride to commemorate the Trail of Tears, the long westward trek of the Cherokee, Muscogee, Seminole, Chickasaw, and Choctaw tribes to the Indian territory of Oklahoma in 1830. Along the way, thousands died of exposure, disease, and starvation. "The Trail of Tears Ride is a fundraiser for the Wounded Warriors Project for recent US military veterans. There is a small powwow at the other end of the ride, but it's mostly white people," Chelle said.[24]

Iraq War veteran David Taptto recently traveled back to Winslow, Arizona, where he has begun to reconnect with his wife and their daughters. His eldest, Gwen, is on her way to college at Northland Pioneer College in Holbrook, Arizona. His middle daughter, Arianna Jo, was recently accepted by Dartmouth College in Hanover, New Hampshire. "That's a big deal," said David. "My youngest daughter, Kristin, is holding down a 3.5 grade point average as a junior and playing all the sports. She has her sights set on UC Irvine. I am very proud of them all."[25]

David has taken time during his recovery from addictions to reflect on his life's journey up to now. "I see a struggle during high school, where I could have easily failed. I look back at another time in my life when I could have easily been dead. Both times, Isabel has been present. Her Upward Bound program provided the means, and she provided the motivation. During my darkest hours, she was always present in the back of my mind. I could always hear her saying, 'You need to get back in school, Dave.' I only hope my daughters can meet this strong woman one day."[26]

O.J. Watters was working as head custodian at the Nez Perce Clearwater River Casino when he provided interviews for this book. He recalled with affection his aunt, Mari Watters, who fought diabetes for many years until the disease disabled her. "Instead of getting her foot cut off, she let the disease progress until she was walking with a cane, and then she was in a wheelchair. Eventually it caused her to pass away," he said.[27] As her illness progressed, Mari Watters dedicated a small section of wheat land to generate money for scholarships for Nez Perce students at U of I. Each year, a new crop is sold, and that money goes to Nez Perce students. O.J. passed away in 2016 at his home in Juliaetta, Idaho. Nez Perce tribal historian, spiritual leader, and author Horace Axtell passed away in 2015.

Mona Daniels continues to work for the Coeur d'Alene Tribe's Child Support Services program. She recently had the opportunity to take in a young member of her family whose circumstances were similar to her own as a child. "Her name is Alizea," said Mona. "She is my niece, and she was raised in foster care since the age of two. I moved home after graduating from UW and attended Eastern Washington University for my master's program so that I could be closer to Spokane and begin fighting for custody of her. Today, I am raising her as a single parent.

She is nine years old and just started fifth grade yesterday. She is doing awesome. She is just such a smart little girl."[28]

Jenny Albert Blackeagle has continued to expand her understanding of Native American law and cultures by taking online courses at UCLA. Since decreasing her intake of popular culture, she has had a renewed interest in Nez Perce traditions that gives her a new perspective on mainstream society. "I feel like the evolution of our society has steered native people from the path of what our ancestors wanted. There is so much societal pressure to fit in to mainstream society and to keep up with the Joneses," Jenny said. "We seem to forget that we are a distinct population of people, older than America and older than the Constitution. There is no one to keep up with. We have only to fulfill what our ancestors expected and wanted. We were never meant to be greedy consumers, but we were meant to take care of the land, animals, and natural resources."[29]

ACKNOWLEDGMENTS

THANKS TO Darlene Dyer for having faith in me to tell this story and to Julie Weston and Charlie Brandt for their mentorship along the way. Thanks to Ron Halfmoon for visiting with me in Lapwai early on and to Dr. Rodney Frey for supporting the manuscript and troubleshooting at the last minute. Thanks to Kim Stafford for inspiration and guidance.

Thanks to the editors at WSU Press—Beth DeWeese for initial support, Robert Clark for knowing where the first chapter was, and Linda Bathgate for carrying it forward. Thanks to Christina Dubois for her final review of the manuscript.

Thanks to the Latah County Museum Society for helpful transcripts of oral histories and to the Community Library in Ketchum for access to research materials. Thanks to Angel Sobotta for details about the Nez Perce language and to Josiah Pinkham for setting me on the road with a detailed guide to the Nez Perce National Historical Park and his own family's inspiring story. Thanks to Professor Elizabeth Fenn, who told me to remember that my work is important and that "Native American History *is* American History."

Thanks to my brother Chris for spiritual guidance and to my other "brothers" for listening to my stories, excitement, and concerns along the way. Thanks to my many excellent teachers, including the uncles, aunts, and cousins at Kahnawake for helping me to understand and respect my own indigenous background and the traditions of other First Nations. Thanks to my mother Tewa, Aunt Nadine, and sister Julie for keeping me laughing. Thank you most of all to my wife Lauren for her love and support; without her presence in my life, I would not have found the faith and dedication to become a writer.

◈ NOTES ◈

INTRODUCTION

1) "Upward Bound Celebrates 50 Years of Opening College Pathways for Underprivileged Students," *Fox News Lifestyle*, July 27, 2014, https://www.foxnews.com/lifestyle/upward-bound-celebrates-50-years-of-opening-college-pathways-for-underprivileged-students.
2) "Famous TRIO," Mt. San Jacinto College, Upward Bound, accessed May 6, 2020, https://ou.msjc.edu/upwardbound/famous-trio.html.
3) "Upward Bound and Upward Bound Math-Science Programs Postsecondary Outcomes Report," US Department of Education, September 2016, https://www2.ed.gov/programs/trioupbound/ub-ubms-outcomes2016.pdf.
4) "Indian Country Demographics," National Congress of American Indians, based on the US Census, 2010 Census Redistricting File, issued January 2011, http://www.ncai.org/about-tribes/demographics.
5) Scott Clyde, Upward Bound demographics based on a 2019 analysis by Darlene Dyer of program yearbooks from 1974 through 1991.
6) Upward Bound yearbooks, Google Drive shared file, last modified June 8, 2018, https://drive.google.com/drive/folders/18XZYEnOURmv5vXNR_9QuI7LevYjAHL7W?usp=sharing.
7) Sylvia R. Epps et al., *Upward Bound at 50: Reporting on Implementation Practices Today*, National Center for Education Evaluation and Regional Assistance, Institute of Education Sciences (Alexandria, VA: US Department of Education, November 2016), https://ies.ed.gov/ncee/pubs/20174005/.
8) Clyde, Upward Bound demographics.

CHAPTER 1

1) Gail Jensen, personal interview with author, June 2014.
2) Sylvia R. Epps et al., *Upward Bound at 50: Reporting on Implementation Practices Today*, National Center for Education Evaluation and Regional Assistance, Institute of Education Sciences (Alexandria, VA: US Department of Education, November 2016), https://ies.ed.gov/ncee/pubs/20174005/.
3) Jensen interview.

4) Jensen interview.
5) Jensen.
6) Dyer interview.
7) Dyer.
8) Dyer.
9) Dyer.
10) Dyer.
11) Dyer.

CHAPTER 2

1) Barbara Austin, "A Paradise Called the Palouse," *National Geographic*, June 1982, 810–11.
2) "Nez Perce (Nee-Me-Poo) National Historic Trail," USDA Forest Service, accessed April 29, 2020, https://www.fs.usda.gov/npnht/.
3) Kim Stafford, "A Few Miles Short of Wisdom," *Having Everything Right: Essays of Place* (Lewiston, ID: Confluence Press, 1986), 32.
4) Stafford, 32.
5) Isabel Bond, personal interview with author, August 2014.

CHAPTER 3

1) "History of the Federal TRIO Programs," US Department of Education, Office of Postsecondary Education, last modified September 9, 2011, https://www2.ed.gov/about/offices/list/ope/trio/triohistory.html.
2) Margalit Fox, "Lloyd E. Ohlin, Expert on Crime and Punishment Is Dead at 90," *New York Times*, January 3, 2009, https://www.nytimes.com/2009/01/04/us/04ohlin.html.
3) "Northern New Mexico Receives $1.28 Million Upward Bound Grant," Northern New Mexico College, June 6, 2017, https://nnmc.edu/northern-new-mexico-college-receives-1-28-million-upward-bound-grant/.
4) "Funding Status—Upward Bound Program," US Department of Education, last modified March 8, 2018, https://www2.ed.gov/programs/trioupbound/funding.html.
5) "Northern New Mexico."
6) Otis Halfmoon, personal interview with author, July 2015.
7) Halfmoon.
8) Halfmoon.
9) Halfmoon.
10) Halfmoon.
11) Kenneth B. Platt, *Centennial 1880–1980: A History of the First Presbyterian Church of Moscow, Idaho* (Moscow: First Presbyterian Church, 1980), 3–5.
12) Platt, *Centennial.*
13) Alvin M. Josephy Jr., *Nez Perce Country* (Lincoln: University of Nebraska Press, 2007), 42.
14) Josephy, 90.
15) Josephy, 98.
16) Josephy, 99.
17) Isabel Bond, personal interview with author, August 2014.
18) Bond.
19) Josephy, *Nez Perce Country*, 57.
20) Bond interview.
21) Bond.

22) Halfmoon interview.
23) Halfmoon.
24) Halfmoon.
25) Halfmoon.
26) Halfmoon.
27) Halfmoon.
28) Halfmoon.
29) Halfmoon.
30) Bond interview.
31) Bond.
32) "Upward Bound and Upward Bound Math-Science Programs Postsecondary Outcomes Report," US Department of Education, September 2016, https://www2.ed.gov/programs/trioupbound/ub-ubms-outcomes2016.pdf.
33) Chris (Mahoney) Meyer, personal interview with author, September 2014.
34) Meyer.
35) Meyer.
36) Meyer.
37) Meyer.
38) Meyer.
39) Meyer.
40) Meyer.
41) Meyer.
42) Halfmoon interview.
43) Halfmoon.

CHAPTER 4

1) Isabel Bond, personal interview with author, August 2014.
2) Bond.
3) Lucinda George, personal interview with author, October 2014.
4) George.
5) George.
6) George.
7) George.
8) George.
9) Caroline James, *Nez Perce Women in Transition, 1877–1990* (Moscow: University of Idaho Press, 1996), 204.
10) Bob Wheaton, personal interview with author, November 2014.
11) Wheaton.
12) Wheaton.
13) Wheaton.
14) Wheaton.
15) Wheaton.
16) Wheaton.
17) Wheaton.
18) George interview, 2014.
19) George.

20) George.
21) Bond interview.
22) Bill Picard, personal interview with author, February 2014.
23) Picard.
24) Picard.
25) Picard.
26) Picard.
27) Bond interview.
28) Bond.
29) Bond.
30) Isabel E. Bond, letter to the editor, *Moscow-Pullman Daily News*, February 1, 2013, https://dnews.com/opinion/good-intentions-misdirected/article_ec89c285-d29a-51bf-b55c-c1599ae73272.html?utm_medium=social&utm_source=email&utm_campaign=user-share.

CHAPTER 5

1) Sam Schrager, "Lola Gamble Clyde," 1975–1976, Latah County Oral History Collection, Digital Initiatives, University of Idaho Library, accessed May 6, 2020, https://www.lib.uidaho.edu/digital/lcoh/people/CLYDE_Lola.html.
2) Schrager.
3) Mychel Matthews, "Albion State Normal School: Training Students to Be Teachers," accessed July 9, 2014, https://magicvalley.com/community/mini-cassia/the-albion-normal-school-training-students-to-be-teachers/article_da8c842e-0591-11e4-b19d-0019bb2963f4.html.
4) Schrager, "Lola Gamble Clyde."
5) Schrager.
6) Schrager.
7) Schrager.
8) Schrager.
9) Schrager.
10) Lola Clyde, reprint of a letter to the editor, *International Harvester World*, March 1965, *Latah Legacy: The Semi-Annual Journal of the Latah County Historical Society* 22, no.1 (Spring 1993), 16, https://210037ce-4f50-408e-b3bf-a053e1bb45bc.filesusr.com/ugd/c533b2_5155f93392b448b1a8f08314ca23f405.pdf.
11) Ronald D. Knutson, David P. Ernstes, and R. J. Hildreth, *Farm Foundation, 75 Years as a Catalyst to Agriculture and Rural America* (Oak Brook, IL: Farm Foundation, 2007), 12.
12) Clyde, reprint.
13) Clyde, reprint.
14) Clyde, reprint.
15) Clyde, reprint.
16) Schrager, "Lola Gamble Clyde."
17) Isabel Bond, personal interview with author, August 2014.
18) "Grace Jain Wicks, 90, Longtime Moscow Columnist," *Lewiston Tribune*, June 20, 1997, https://lmtribune.com/obituaries/grace-jain-wicks-longtime-moscow-columnist/article_a5136fd5-41eb-5f30-a154-4b0712fc0848.html.
19) Wicks.

20) Sam Schrager, "Gus Gamble," 1974, Latah County Oral History Collection, Digital Initiatives, University of Idaho Library, accessed May 6, 2020, https://www.lib.uidaho.edu/digital/lcoh/people/gamble_gus.html.
21) David Wahl, personal interview with author, March 2016.
22) Wahl.
23) Wahl.
24) Wahl.
25) "Jackson Sundown," USDA Forest Service, Nez Perce (Nee-Me-Poo) National Historic Trail, accessed May 6, 2020, https://www.fs.usda.gov/detail/npnht/learningcenter/history-culture/?cid=fseprd539250.
26) Wahl interview.
27) Wahl.
28) Wahl.
29) Jamie Francis, "Round-Up Then and Now: Jackson Sundown," *Oregonian*, September 14, 2010 (updated January 10, 2019), https://www.oregonlive.com/pacific-northwest-news/2010/09/round-up_then_and_now_jackson_sundown.html.
30) Jackson "Waaya Tonah Tolsits Kahn" Sundown, photograph of Jackson Sundown's gravestone inscription, accessed May 6, 2020, https://www.findagrave.com/memorial/45528781/jackson-sundown#view-photo=28982512.
31) David Wahl, "Sundown" (poem), *The Illustrated Mist in the Wind* (Genesee, ID: Brooklawn Books, 2003), reprinted with permission of the author.
32) Grace Wicks, "Remembering Gus Gamble," *The Idahonian* (November, 28, 1978), 4.
33) Wahl interview.
34) Wahl.
35) Wicks, "Remembering Gus Gamble," 4.
36) Wicks, 4.
37) Wicks, 4.
38) Schrager, "Lola Gamble Clyde."
39) Schrager.
40) "Lola Gamble Clyde," *Legendary Locals of Moscow Idaho* (Moscow, ID: Latah County Historical Society, 2015), 55.
41) Barbara Austin, "A Paradise Called the Palouse," *National Geographic*, June 1982, 810–11.
42) Dan Rather, "Lola Clyde Interview," CBS News, December 8, 1987.

CHAPTER 6

1) "Allotment Act – 1887," History and Culture, Partnership with Native Americans, accessed May 6, 2020, http://www.nativepartnership.org/site/PageServer?pagename=PWNA_Native_History_allotmentactNP.
2) Isabel Bond, personal interview with author, August 2014.
3) Mark R. Scherer, "Dawes Act," Encyclopedia of the Great Plains, University of Nebraska Lincoln, accessed May 6, 2020, http://plainshumanities.unl.edu/encyclopedia/doc/egp.law.015.
4) Stacy Thacker, "Nez Perce Launches First Part of Land Buyback Program," *Lewiston Tribune*, July 30, 2016, https://lmtribune.com/northwest/nez-perce-tribe-launches-first-part-of-land-buyback-program/article_9d656f22-3ff9-5d95-b3c1-46d5d525ebfe.html.
5) Phillip Allen, personal interview with author, March 2016.
6) Allen.

7) Allen.
8) Allen.
9) Allen.
10) Allen.
11) Allen.
12) "The Spalding Site," Nez Perce National Historic Park, National Park Service, US Department of the Interior, updated November 25, 2017, https://www.nps.gov/nepe/learn/historyculture/the-spalding-site.htm.
13) Jack McNeel, "10 Things You Should Know About the Nez Perce Tribe," *Indian Country Today*, April 12, 2017, https://newsmaven.io/indiancountrytoday/archive/10-things-you-should-know-about-the-nez-perce-tribe-bFbKNrLV6kCvHNe7Eyhc7w/.
14) "Nez Perce Water Settlement to be Implemented," Native American Rights Fund, Water Rights, April 27, 2007, https://www.narf.org/nez-perce-water-settlement-to-be-implemented/.
15) Patrick Impero Wilson, "Wolves, Politics, and the Nez Perce: Wolf Recovery in Central Idaho and the Role of Native Tribes," *Natural Resources Journal*, Summer 1999, http://digitalrepository.unm.edu/cgi/viewcontent.cgi?article=1650&context=nrj.
16) Tim Woodward, "Nez Perce Honors 'Warriors' Who Fought for Fishing Rights," *Idaho Statesman*, June 9, 2005, http://www.bluefish.org/warriors.htm.
17) "National Park Service visitation tops 318 million in 2018," National Park Service, Office of Communications, March 5, 2019, https://www.nps.gov/orgs/1207/03-05-2019-visitation-numbers.htm.
18) "Visit Bear Paw Battlefield," Nez Perce National Historic Park, National Park Service, US Department of the Interior, updated February 17, 2018, https://www.nps.gov/nepe/planyourvisit/visit-bear-paw-battlefield.htm.
19) Pete Wilson, personal interview with author, October 2016.
20) Wilson.
21) Wilson.
22) Wilson.
23) Wilson.
24) Wilson.
25) Bond interview.
26) Bond.
27) Bond.
28) Darlene (Matson) Dyer, personal interview with author, June 2014.

CHAPTER 7

1) Elinor Michel, personal interview with author, August 2015.
2) Michel.
3) Michel.
4) Darlene (Matson) Dyer, personal interview with author, June 2014.
5) Dyer.
6) Gail Jensen, personal interview with author, June 2014.
7) Robert Seward, personal interview with author, August 2015.
8) Seward.
9) Seward.
10) Seward.

11) Seward.
12) Seward.
13) Glenn Williams, personal interview with author, August 2015.
14) Williams.
15) Williams.
16) Williams.
17) Williams.
18) Ollicutt "O.J." Watters, personal interview with author, August 2015.
19) Dyer interview.
20) Dyer.
21) Dyer.
22) Isabel Bond, personal interview with author, August 2014.
23) Brad Filkins, personal interview with author, October 2015.
24) Filkins.
25) Filkins.
26) Filkins.
27) Filkins.
28) Filkins.
29) Filkins.
30) Filkins.
31) Dyer interview.
32) Dyer.

CHAPTER 8

1) Darlene (Matson) Dyer, personal interview with author, June 2014.
2) Dyer.
3) "Monday Night Sports at Upward Bound," *Taats Timeepnin Tyum*, 1988 Upward Bound yearbook (Moscow: University of Idaho, 1988), 15, accessed May 6, 2020, https://drive.google.com/drive/folders/18XZYEnOURmv5vXNR_9QuI7LevYjAHL7W.
4) Dyer interview.
5) Dyer.
6) Isabel Bond, personal interview with author, August 2014.
7) Ollicutt "O.J." Watters, personal interview with author, August 2015.
8) Bond interview.
9) Bond.
10) Tana Wheeler, personal interview with author, November 2015.
11) Wheeler.
12) Ralph Bartholdt, "Nez Perce Elder Horace P. Axtell Dies at Age 90," *Lewiston Tribune*, September 8, 2015, https://lmtribune.com/northwest/nez-perce-elder-horace-p-axtell-dies-at-age/article_a28fc5d3-e5bd-5279-8071-8a2486b02553.html.
13) Anne Wilson Schaef, *Native Wisdom for White Minds: Daily Reflections Inspired by the Native Peoples of the World* (New York: One World/Penguin Random House, 1995), November 19.
14) Jack McNeel, "Horace Axtell – World War II Vet and Ceremonial Leader," February 20, 2012, *Indian Country Today*, https://indiancountrytoday.com/archive/horace-axtell-world-war-ii-vet-and-ceremonial-leader-KDUajQNPJ0yt0pmqi4xh_g.
15) Rudy Boesch, personal interview with author, July 2015.

16) Boesch.
17) *Nez Perce Country: A Handbook for Nez Perce National Historical Park, Idaho*, National Park Service, Division of Publications (Washington, DC: US Department of Interior, 1983), 53–54, https://babel.hathitrust.org/cgi/pt?id=pur1.32754061600262&view=1up&seq=53.
18) Family Tree Collection, a Potlatch Forests, Inc. Newsletter, Digital Initiatives, University of Idaho Library, updated September 18, 2019, https://www.lib.uidaho.edu/digital/familytree/about.html.
19) Bond interview.
20) Wheeler interview.
21) "Weiss Rockshelter," Nez Perce National Historic Park, National Park Service, US Department of the Interior, updated November 6, 2017, https://www.nps.gov/nepe/learn/historyculture/weis-rockshelter.htm.
22) *Nez Perce Country*, 118.
23) Chief Joseph, "An Indian's View of Indian Affairs," excerpted from *North American Review*, April 1879, 419–20, Center for the Study of the Pacific Northwest, University of Washington, accessed May 6, 2020, https://www.washington.edu/uwired/outreach/cspn/Website/Classroom%20Materials/Reading%20the%20Region/Texts%20by%20and%20about%20Natives/Texts/9.html.
24) Merrill D. Beal, *I Will Fight No More Forever: Chief Joseph and the Nez Perce War* (Seattle: University of Washington Press, 1985), 43.
25) Beal, 45.
26) Beal, 50.
27) Beal, 52.
28) Beal, 53.
29) Lucullus Virgil McWhorter, *Yellow Wolf: His Own Words* (Caldwell, ID: Caxton Press, 1983), 134.
30) McWhorter, 134.
31) Beal, 65.
32) McWhorter, 135.
33) Boesch interview.
34) Boesch.
35) Text from a historical Lolo Trail marker commemorating the Lewis and Clark expedition, near US Highway 12 and the mouth of Fish Creek, accessed May 6, 2020, https://www.waymarking.com/gallery/default.aspx?f=1&guid=115860bf-bf28-4dd7-9f11-6a88be734d7e&gid=2.
36) Meriwether Lewis and William Clark, *The Lewis and Clark Journals: An American Epic of Discovery*, ed. by Gary E. Moulton (Lincoln: University of Nebraska Press, 2003), 396.
37) Meriwether Lewis and William Clark, *The Essential Lewis and Clark*, ed. by Anthony Brandt (Washington, DC: National Geographic Books, 2002), 389.
38) McWhorter, 181.
39) Beal, 115.
40) Beal, 137.
41) Beal, 138.
42) Kim Stafford, "A Few Miles Short of Wisdom," *Having Everything Right: Essays of Place* (Lewiston, ID: Confluence Press, 1986), 27.
43) McWhorter, 126.
44) Stafford, 31.

45) Elliott West, *The Last Indian War: The Nez Perce Story, Pivotal Moments in History* (New York: Oxford University Press, 2009), 196.
46) Stafford, 32.
47) Stafford, 32.
48) McWhorter, 134.
49) McWhorter, 135.
50) McWhorter, 135.
51) McWhorter, 138.
52) McWhorter, 138.
53) McWhorter, 137.
54) Josiah Pinkham, personal interview with author, August 2016.
55) Bond interview.
56) Janet Torline, personal interview with author, 2019.
57) McWhorter, 188–89.
58) Beal, 255.
59) Pinkham interview.
60) McWhorter, 135.
61) Grant Adair to Isabel Bond, June 18, 1988, private collection.
62) Ken Brown, "Anti-Apartheid Protests Waning, Students Fight Racism on Campus," United Press International, UPI Archives, May 29, 1988, https://www.upi.com/Archives/1988/05/29/Anti-apartheid-protests-waning-Students-fight-racism-on-campus/2972580881600/.
63) Penwell Dlamini, "Sharpeville Massacre: Survivors Say Their Dreams of Better Days are Fading," *Sunday Times*, Times Live, South Africa, March 21, 2018, https://www.timeslive.co.za/news/south-africa/2018-03-21-sharpeville-massacre-survivors-say-their-dreams-of-better-days-are-fading/.
64) Albert Penney to President P. W. Botha, *Taats Timeepnin Tyum*, 1988 Upward Bound yearbook (Moscow: University of Idaho, 1988), 38, accessed May 6, 2020, https://drive.google.com/drive/folders/18XZYEnOURmv5vXNR_9QuI7LevYjAHL7W.
65) *Taats Timeepnin Tyum*, 1988 Upward Bound yearbook (Moscow: University of Idaho, 1988), 1 and 19, accessed May 6, 2020, https://drive.google.com/drive/folders/18XZYEnOURmv5vXNR_9QuI7LevYjAHL7W.
66) Dyer interview and personal writing.
67) Dyer interview.
68) Greg Torline, personal interview with author, 2019.

CHAPTER 9

1) Ollicutt "O.J." Watters, personal interview with author, August 2015.
2) Bruce E. Johansen, *Resource Exploitation in Native America: A Plague Upon the Peoples* (Santa Barbara: Praeger Publishing, 2016), 22.
3) Watters interview.
4) Watters.
5) Watters.
6) Watters.
7) "Missionaries and Christianity," Nez Perce Culture, Lifelong Learning Online: The Lewis and Clark Rediscovery Project, 2002, accessed November 2019, https://www.lib.uidaho.edu/digital/L3/ShowOneObjectSiteID34ObjectID97.html.

8) Wilma Lawrence, personal interview with author, August 2015.
9) Lawrence interview.
10) Lawrence.
11) Josiah Pinkham, personal interview with author, August 2016.
12) Wyatt Buchanan, "Tribal Ethnographer Passes on Heritage to Younger Generations," Nez Perce Tribe, Idaho Natives, accessed May 6, 2020, http://www.buffalogirlsproductions.com/idahonatives/nez/ethno.html.
13) Pinkham interview.
14) Pinkham.
15) Pinkham.
16) Francis Haines, "The Northward Spread of Horses among the Plains Indians," *American Anthropologist*, July–September 1938, https://doi.org/10.1525/aa.1938.40.3.02a00060, 431.
17) Pinkham interview.
18) Pinkham.
19) Pinkham.
20) Pinkham.
21) Pinkham.

CHAPTER 10

1) Suzzanne Penney, personal interview with author, September 2014.
2) Suzzanne Penney interview.
3) "Welcome - Ta'c Haláxp," Kate and Sue McBeth: Missionary Teachers to the Nez Perce, University of Idaho Library, last updated April 24, 2000, https://www.lib.uidaho.edu/mcbeth/welcome.htm.
4) Luke Penney, personal interview with author, September 2014.
5) Editors of Encyclopaedia Britannica, "Dawes General Allotment Act," *Encyclopaedia Britannica*, last updated December 4, 2019, https://www.britannica.com/topic/Dawes-General-Allotment-Act.
6) Luke Penney interview.
7) Luke Penney.
8) Suzzanne Penney interview.
9) Luke Penney interview.
10) Luke Penney.
11) Suzzanne Penney interview.
12) Luke Penney interview.
13) Luke Penney.
14) Luke Penney.
15) Luke Penney.
16) Luke Penney.
17) Luke Penney.
18) Mark Cheater, "Wolf Spirit Returns to Idaho," *National Wildlife*, August 1, 1998, https://www.nwf.org/en/Magazines/National-Wildlife/1998/Wolf-Spirit-Returns-to-Idaho.
19) Luke Penney interview.

CHAPTER 11

1) Mary Taylor, personal interview with author, September 2014.
2) Taylor.

3) Taylor.
4) Taylor.
5) Taylor.
6) Taylor.
7) Mabel "Robin" Black Eagle, personal interview with author, September 2014.
8) Black Eagle.
9) Black Eagle.
10) Black Eagle.
11) Black Eagle.
12) Black Eagle.
13) Black Eagle.
14) Black Eagle.
15) Black Eagle.
16) Black Eagle.
17) Editors of Encyclopaedia Britannica, "Indian Reorganization Act," *Encyclopaedia Britannica*, October 10, 2016, https://www.britannica.com/topic/Indian-Reorganization-Act.
18) "Indian Self-Determination and Education Assistance Act – 1975," Partnership with Native Americans, Resources, History and Culture, accessed May 6, 2020, http://www.nativepartnership.org/site/PageServer?pagename=PWNA_Native_History_selfdeterminationactNP.
19) Black Eagle interview.
20) Black Eagle.
21) Chelle-Rene (Merrill) Josefowicz, personal interview with author, September 2014.
22) Josefowicz.
23) Josefowicz.
24) Josefowicz.
25) Josefowicz.
26) Josefowicz.
27) Josefowicz.
28) Josefowicz.
29) Josefowicz.
30) Jenny Albert Blackeagle, personal interview with author, January 2015.
31) Blackeagle.
32) Blackeagle.
33) Blackeagle.
34) Blackeagle.
35) Blackeagle.
36) Blackeagle.

CHAPTER 12

1) Darlene (Matson) Dyer, personal interview with author, June 2014.
2) "Ma'amin, the Nez Perce Horse," AAA Native Arts, Culture and Tribal Customs, Native American Animals, accessed May 6, 2010, https://www.aaanativearts.com/maamin-the-nez-perce-horse.
3) Michael Murphy, "Nez Perce Launch Horse Breeding Program," Articles, Nez Perce Horse Registry, November 1995, http://www.nezpercehorseregistry.com/articles.html.

4) Dan McComb, "Cultural Classroom: A New Program Teaches Nez Perce Traditions to Troubled Youths," *Spokesman-Review*, August 17, 1997, https://www.spokesman.com/stories/1997/aug/17/cultural-classroom-a-new-program-teaches-nez/.
5) Lucinda George, personal interview with author, September 2015.
6) George, 2015.
7) Jim Robbins, "Tribe Famous for Horses Sees Future in Them," *New York Times*, November 3, 1996, https://www.nytimes.com/1996/11/03/us/tribe-famous-for-horses-sees-future-in-them.html.
8) Robbins.
9) "Major Donors," Chief Joseph Foundation, accessed May 6, 2020, http://chiefjosephfoundation.org/major-doners-and-partners/.
10) "Lillian Disney Dies: Philanthropist Widow of Walt Disney Remembered Her Idaho Roots," *Spokesman-Review*, December 18, 1997, https://www.spokesman.com/stories/1997/dec/18/lillian-disney-dies-philanthropist-widow-of-walt/.
11) Jocelyn Pierce, "The Chief Joseph Trail Ride," *Equitrekking*, June 2, 2017, https://equitrekking.com/articles/entry/the-chief-joseph-trail-ride.
12) "Testimonials from Participants," Chief Joseph Foundation, http://chiefjosephfoundation.org/history/testimonials-from-participants/.
13) "Testimonials."
14) Connie Fleener, personal interview with author, November 2016.
15) Fleener.
16) Fleener.
17) Fleener.
18) Fleener.
19) Fleener.
20) Fleener.
21) Fleener.
22) Fleener.
23) Quoted text by Vine Deloria Jr., American Indian Science and Engineering Society (AISES) 1994 conference catalog, 31.
24) Sydel Samuels, personal interview with author, October 2016.
25) Sydel Samuels.
26) Sydel Samuels.
27) Sydel Samuels.
28) Sydel Samuels.
29) Sydel Samuels.
30) Jessica Samuels, personal interview with author, September 2014.
31) Jessica Samuels.
32) Jessica Samuels.
33) Jessica Samuels.
34) Jessica Samuels.
35) Jessica Samuels.
36) Jessica Samuels.
37) Jessica Samuels.
38) Jessica Samuels.

CHAPTER 13

1) Mona Daniels, personal interview with author, June 2014.
2) Daniels.
3) Daniels.
4) Daniels.
5) Daniels.
6) Daniels.
7) Daniels.
8) Daniels.
9) David Taptto, personal interview with author, August 2015.
10) Taptto.
11) Taptto.
12) Taptto.
13) Taptto.
14) Taptto.
15) Taptto.
16) Taptto.
17) Taptto.
18) Taptto.
19) Taptto.
20) Taptto.
21) Taptto.
22) Taptto.
23) Taptto.
24) Taptto.
25) Taptto.

EPILOGUE

1) Shawn Vestal, "Advocate for Native students fighting UI," *Spokesman-Review*, October 18, 2005, https://www.spokesman.com/stories/2005/oct/18/advocate-for-native-students-fighting-ui/
2) Vestal.
3) Vestal.
4) Camille Wynecoop, personal interview with author, May 10, 2020.
5) Scott Clyde, personal interview with author, May 17, 2020.
6) Clyde.
7) Clyde.
8) Clyde.
9) Chris (Mahoney) Meyer, personal interview with author, September 2014.
10) Otis Halfmoon, personal interview with author, July 2015.
11) Bob Wheaton, personal interview with author, November 2014.
12) Wheaton.
13) Wheaton.
14) Wheaton.
15) Wheaton.
16) Bill Picard, personal interview with author, February 2014.

17) Picard.
18) Picard.
19) Lucinda George, personal interview with author, September 2015.
20) George.
21) Robert Seward, personal interview with author, August 2015.
22) Seward.
23) Chelle-Rene (Merrill) Josefowicz, personal interview with author, September 2014.
24) Josefowicz.
25) David Taptto, personal interview with author, August 2015.
26) Taptto.
27) Ollicutt "O.J." Watters, personal interview with author, August 2015.
28) Mona Daniels, personal interview with author, June 2014.
29) Jenny Albert Blackeagle, personal interview with author, January 2015.

INDEX